The **Jumbo**
Book of Magic Tricks

The JUMBO! BOOK of MAGIC TRICKS

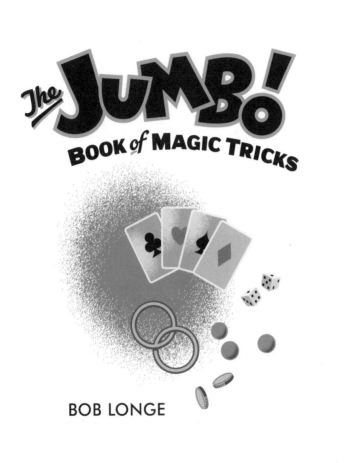

BOB LONGE

Sterling Publishing Co., Inc.
New York

**Library of Congress Cataloging-in-Publication
Data Available**

10   9   8   7   6   5   4   3   2   1

Published in 2005 by Sterling Publishing Co., Inc.
387 Park Avenue South, New York, NY 10016
First published in 1999 by Sterling Publishing Co., Inc.
under the title *The Little Giant Encyclopedia of Magic*
Copyright © 1999 by Bob Longe
Distributed in Canada by Sterling Publishing
℅ Canadian Manda Group, 165 Dufferin Street
Toronto, Ontario, Canada M6K 3H6
Distributed in Great Britain and Europe by
Chris Lloyd at Orca Book Service
Stanley House, Fleets Lane, Poole BH15 3AJ, England
Distributed in Australia by Capricorn Link (Australia) Pty Ltd.
P.O. Box 704, Windsor, NSW 2756, Australia

Sterling ISBN 1-4027-1779-2

Contents

Introduction

Perhaps in some magic books you've found the same familiar material. You're forced to ask yourself, "How about something new, different, exciting, entertaining, or clever?" Here you have all of that.

The vast majority of the tricks are impromptu, and those that aren't require very little preparation. And what a variety you have! You'll find tricks with coins, folding money, dice, playing cards, handkerchiefs, rubber bands, string, rope, thimbles, tableware, pencils, calendars, and miscellaneous objects. And with the clear instructions provided, you can perform mental magic, amazing feats with numbers, and real prestidigitation—that is, tricks using only your fingers. Furthermore, you can provide fascinating examples of "hypnotism."

Best of all, no trick is beyond your grasp. Here you'll not find impossible sleights, requiring hundreds of hours of practice; instead, the emphasis is on ease of handling. What's the good of knowing dozens of wonderful tricks if they are too difficult to perform? With some practice and proper application, every trick here can be mastered, and you'll have several mystifying routines available at your fingertips.

Do you already know several magic tricks? We may have

some of those here also, but with new presentation points, lively patter, and superior methods.

The whole point to performing magic is to provide entertainment. This book provides the tools, but *you* must be the craftsman. Your thoughtful practice, with both patter and technique, will pay off with clear audience approval.

A Few Pointers

S ome stand-up comics treat the audience as though they are opponents. Occasionally, this can be amusing, but usually—at least for me—it's quite annoying. Some magicians make this same mistake: They feel as though they're competing with the audience and that they must win at any cost.

When you perform magic, remember that the spectators are not your enemies, so don't treat them that way.

Of course there are obnoxious spectators. They can be put into several categories: (1) the loudmouths who think people will be amused at their stupid comments; (2) the compulsive know-it-alls, who are quite sure they know exactly how each trick was done, and when they don't know—which is most of the time—speak in their native language, "Dahhh, I know dat one"; (3) the spoilers, who try to foul up the tricks by failing to follow directions; (4) the grabbers, who try to grasp the magician's hand to see if there is anything hidden there; (5) the show-offs, who resent the fact that they are not the center of attention; and (6), the arrogant spectators, who absolutely hate to be fooled and ask questions like, "Why did you take that pile?" or, "What's in your other hand?"

And there are many more annoying types. I have a very good friend, for instance, to whom I'll occasionally show a trick I'm working on. He usually tries to ruin the trick. For instance, if I'm stupid enough to give him a deck of cards, turn my back, and give him instructions, he'll do something a little different. Since he's not a bad person, I can only conclude that he thinks I might really have magical powers and, therefore, is testing me. If so, it's a compliment I could do without.

What's the best way to treat obnoxious spectators? Ignore them. If a person gets really obnoxious, chances are others will shut him up. Don't get angry. Remain composed and friendly.

No matter what the annoyance, ignore it. Relax and enjoy yourself. If it's fun for you, it should be fun for others. As far as I'm concerned, if it's not fun for you, why in the world are you doing it? Actually, I know the answer. Several magicians I know perform primarily to prove how slick they are. And—dare I say it?—some are more obnoxious than any spectator could possibly be.

But there is no need to be concerned with such unpleasantness. You're out to perform good magic and, in the process, to provide entertainment for others and enjoyment for yourself. And if a trick goes wrong, you'll laugh it off, or perhaps pretend that it was your intention to goof up. At the end of your show, the audience will agree that you're a wonderful performer (and maybe even a wonderful magician) and will welcome the chance to see you perform again.

Coins

Obviously, coins are generally available, so it behooves the aspiring magician to be ready to perform a number of good coin tricks. Part I contains tricks that use so-called sleight of hand, requiring some practice. But most are fairly easy, and anything can be learned with a little desire and some application.

First, you'll learn two methods of concealing a coin (the Regular Palm and the Finger Palm), and then a good trick to open with. Next, you'll learn several coin vanishes and reappearances. Then comes a rich variety of coin tricks, depending only on your mastery to provide strong entertainment.

In Part II, the tricks call for no sleight of hand, but still require some practice. For the most part, these tricks involve subtlety, misdirection, and unusual techniques.

Coin Trick Tips

For any maneuver with coins, practice by alternating the natural move and then the trick move. For instance, pretend to place a coin in the left hand, but actually retain it in the right hand. To do this, first place the coin in your left hand. Then perform your trick move, trying to make it exactly like the natural move. When you think you're performing the trick perfectly, take a look in the mirror to make sure that the natural move and the trick move look exactly alike.

When working with coins, the magician frequently seems to transfer a coin from one hand to the other. A thoughtful spectator might just wonder why he's doing this. Why does the coin have to be in the other hand? Fortunately for you and me, there's a rich tradition, especially with coins, of magicians simply transferring objects from one hand to the other without the need to explain why. Nevertheless, it's probably better to have some apparent reason for doing so.

It used to be that the magician would seem to place a coin in his left hand, and then with his right hand reach into the side pocket for some invisible and magical "woofle" dust. The coin would be left in the pocket and the invisible dust sprinkled on the left hand, which was then opened, showing that the coin had disappeared. I don't think that any responsible magician has used the old "woofle" dust ploy for decades. Still, there should be some reason for the transference, shouldn't there?

Certainly. And there are many possibilities. For example, someone who's standing on your right is not quite close enough. You casually transfer the coin from the right hand to your left, or seem to. Then, with the right hand, you wave the spectator on your right to move in closer. Or you actually take his arm and gently move him in closer.

Again, you transfer the coin and then brush back the unruly hair on the right side of your head. Or, with your right hand, you scratch the side of your left arm. Other moves would be to push your glasses back, or remove them, or to point to someone on the right side, saying, "I'll bet you've seen this before." And on and on. I'm sure you can think of several that would be perfect for you.

Part 1

The Regular Palm

Why do I call this "the Regular Palm"? In magic, the word "palm" is used to describe many ways to conceal something in a magician's hand. In this instance, the object—a coin—is actually concealed in the palm.

This palm is very easy, as you'll see. Take a large coin and place it in the palm of your right hand. Cup the hand slightly (Illus. 1). Notice that you are now gripping the coin

Illus .1

quite securely. If you continue holding your hand in this natural way, no one will suspect that a coin is being concealed. Incidentally, you'll soon discover that the smaller the coin, the more your hand will be cupped.

Quite often when you're holding a coin like this, your hand should drop to your side. In a sense, forget that you're holding a coin. The idea is not to be self-conscious about it. I realize that this is a bit like telling someone, "Don't think of a pink elephant," but the key to an effective palm is that your hands, arms—in fact, your entire body—should look natural.

The Finger Palm

The Finger Palm is a standard method for concealing a coin. It's quite easy and very effective. To get the feel for this, take a coin of any size and grip it in the right hand with the second and third fingers (Illus. 2). Note how the coin is secured in the cupped fingers. This slight cupping serves both to grip the coin and provide a natural appearance (Illus. 3).

As above, to achieve the natural look, try to forget that you're holding a coin. Incidentally, this modest sleight is useful for concealing many objects other than coins.

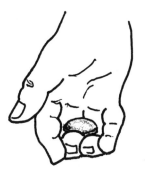

Illus. 2

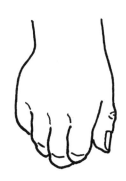

Illus. 3

To Begin With

To perform this excellent trick, you must be familiar with the finger palm, described above. The coin does not disappear or reappear; actually, this trick is an excellent way to begin a series of coin manipulations. Apparently your hands are empty, and then suddenly you're holding a coin.

Start by finger-palming a fairly large coin in the right

hand. Of course, the audience or group should be unaware of this. Turn to the left a quarter-turn. Show both sides of the left hand and wiggle the fingers. At the same time, point the first finger of your right hand at the left hand (Illus. 4).

Swing around so that you're standing a quarter-turn to the right. While doing so, move your left hand under the

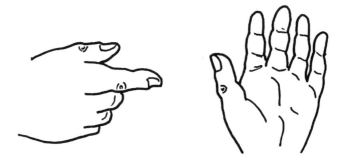

Illus. 4

right, dropping the coin from your right hand to the left (Illus. 5). Show the right hand in exactly the same way as you showed the left: show both sides and wiggle the fingers. Also, at the same time, point with the left first finger at the right hand.

All that remains is to produce the coin. I like the method I developed: After showing the right hand empty, turn it

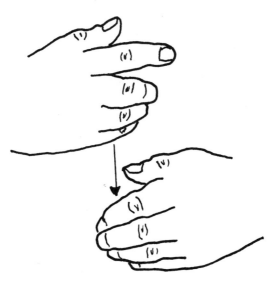

Illus. 5

palm up and pretend to be bouncing a coin on the palm a
few times. Tip the hand forward a bit, presumably moving
the coin toward the fingers. Grasp the invisible coin
between the thumb and fingers and hold it up for all to see
(Illus. 6).

Illus. 6

"Ladies and gentlemen, I'd like you to watch closely as I perform a little stunt with this coin."

Bring your left hand up so that it's just slightly below head level. In the process, the coin will drop into the palm of your left hand. But, of course, no one can see it there.

Bring the right hand over and place the invisible coin into the left palm (Illus. 7). Make sure you close your left fingers as you move the right hand away.

Lower your left hand to belt level.

"Now, with just three quick moves, I'll make the coin disappear." Move your left fist up and down three times.

Open your left hand. Lower it so that all can see the coin.

Maneuver the coin so that you can take it by the left finger-tips. Hold the coin up, saying, "Darn it! I was hoping it would disappear." Pause a moment. "Let's try something else."

Proceed with another coin trick.

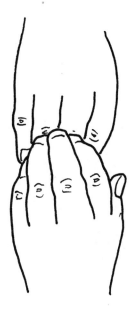

Illus. 7

A Common Vanish

Start by holding out the left hand palm up and displaying a coin on your right fingertips (Illus. 8). Notice that the coin does not overlap the fingertips; this is important.

Place your right thumb on top of the coin, securing it in the right hand (Illus. 9). Tilt the left hand back a bit as you turn the right hand palm down and bring it forward of the left hand and above it. The tips of the right fingers should be lightly touching the fingernails of the left hand (Illus. 10).

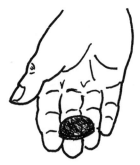

Illus. 8

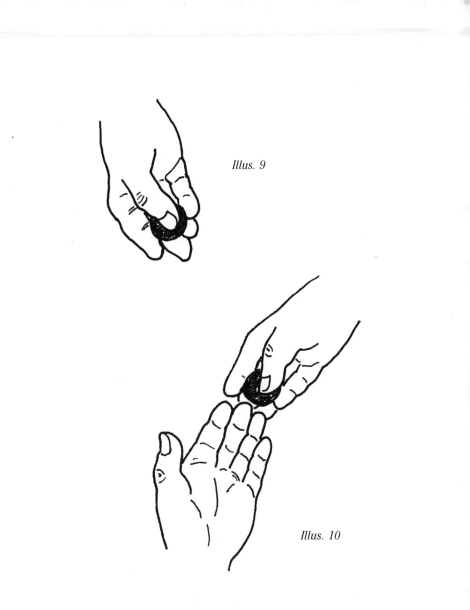

Illus. 9

Illus. 10

Bring your right hand toward you, more or less closing up the left hand by gently pushing the fingers back and, presumably, dropping the coin in the process. But, of course, you're not dropping the coin; you're still retaining your thumb grip.

Keep looking at your left hand as you drop the right hand to your side. When your right hand is about midway in its descent to your side, you can release the thumb grip because the coin will naturally fall onto your semicupped fingers. By cupping your fingers a bit more, you'll find that you are gripping the coin in a *finger palm*.

Flip Vanish

This Milt Kort invention is a very clever change of pace from more conventional vanishes.

Tell the audience, "I'd like to show you something very mysterious. Centuries ago in China, a sorcerer discovered that if you handle a coin in this peculiar way, something strange will happen."

Place a coin onto the tips of the right fingers. Put your left hand onto the right palm (Illus. 11).

Illus. 11

Move both hands upward in a quick movement, flipping the coin into the palm of the left hand. The move is not at all difficult; it can probably be accomplished on your first attempt.

Revolve your left hand clockwise, starting to close it. As you do so, drop the coin onto the right fingers (Illus. 12). Close your left hand completely.

Illus. 12

As soon as the coin hits the right fingers, turn the right hand counterclockwise and close the second, third, and fourth fingers over the coin. Extend the right forefinger, pointing it at the closed left hand (Illus. 13).

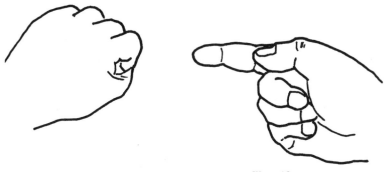

Illus. 13

Show that the coin has vanished, and then make it reappear.

This move is not "angle-proof," meaning that unless you place yourself in a particular position in relation to the audience, someone might see the move. Therefore, after working on the move for a while, do it in front of a mirror to make sure you know what position you should take in relation to the audience.

Small Coin Vanish

S ome time ago, I tried David Ginn's method for making a small coin vanish, but found it quite difficult. So I worked out a simplified method that works well for me.

I think the sleight becomes quite easy if we go through the individual steps:

(1) Hold the left hand out, palm up.

(2) Also hold the right hand out, palm up, with a small coin balanced on the first finger and the other fingers closed up (Illus. 14). Note that the thumb is pressed against the side of the second finger.

Illus. 14

(3) Place the right first finger on the palm of the left hand (Illus. 15).

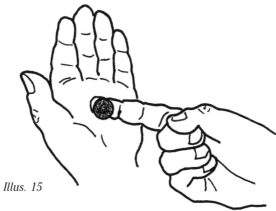

Illus. 15

(4) Turn the left hand clockwise, loosely cupping it as you do so (Illus. 16).

Illus. 16

(5) As soon as the left hand conceals the first finger of the right hand, revolve the right hand slightly in a counter-clockwise direction. At the same time, bend the first finger of the right hand inward. This enables you to press on the coin with your right thumb (Illus. 17).

(6) The right thumb proceeds to slide the coin to the right until it is concealed behind the right fingers. (The arrow in Illus. 18 indicates where the coin is hidden.) At the same time, the left hand closes completely and moves away to the left, presumably taking the coin with it.

(7) Follow your left hand with your eyes as you let the right hand drop to your side and the coin fall into your slightly cupped fingers.

Blow on the closed left hand and then open it to show that the coin has vanished.

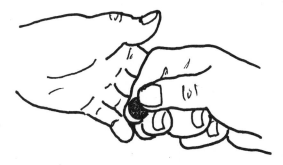

Illus. 17

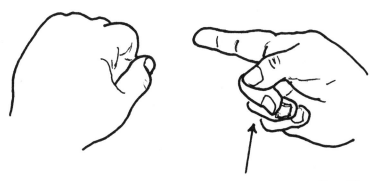

Illus. 18

Making a Coin Reappear

For the most part, every time a coin disappears, it must also reappear. It doesn't much matter where it reappears, but it better show up and soon. Even the dullest observer will eventually figure out that if the coin is not in one hand, it just might be in the other. So after you cause a coin to vanish, bring it back. Produce it from someone's ear, from behind your knee, from your pants pocket, whatever. Keep this in mind while studying the following reappearances.

It's a Toss-Up

You have very cleverly pretended to place a coin in your left hand, whereas it remained in your right hand. Your eyes are locked onto your left hand. Suddenly you throw the invisible coin high into the air. Follow its progress with your eyes as it moves toward the ceiling and then descends. Reach out and catch it in your right hand, and then show it at your right fingertips.

Good Catch

Again the left hand is empty, though everyone thinks it contains a coin. The coin is actually palmed in the right hand, which is hanging at your side. Say a magic word or two and then show everyone that the coin has disappeared from the left hand. Suddenly stare off to your left.

"What's that?" you blurt out.

Reach out your left hand and grab the invisible coin that you've been staring at.

Hold your right hand out palm up, but tilted so that the audience cannot see the palm. Bring the left hand above the right a few inches and open the fingers, dropping the invisible coin into your right palm. Immediately bounce the coin on the right palm a few times and then hold it up at the right fingertips.

From Ear to Ear

You seem to have placed the coin into the left hand, but actually have retained it in the right hand. Now you apparently stick the coin into one ear, and then pull it out of the other.

There are many techniques that can be used, but here's one that works well. Let's say that Peter is standing, facing the group. You move behind him, and also face the group. Your left hand evidently holds the coin between the thumb and the fingertips. The back of the hand is toward the group. Reach over so that the left hand almost touches his left ear (Illus. 19). Pull your thumb back as you push the fingers forward, creating the illusion that you're pushing something into the ear.

Immediately bring your right hand close to his left ear, with the back of the hand toward the group. The coin is held between the thumb and fingertips, but make sure the coin does not project beyond your fingertips.

Now perform an action that is almost the reverse of what you did with the other ear. Draw your fingers back while pushing the coin forward with your thumb (Illus. 20). The coin comes into sight, as though withdrawn from the ear.

Hold the coin up for a moment, displaying it, and then bounce it on your palm a few times so that all can see that it actually is the coin.

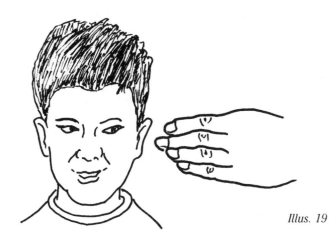

Illus. 19

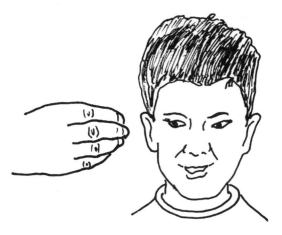

Illus. 20

35

"Oh, Here It Is!"

E vidently you placed a coin into your left hand; actually, you retained it in your right. Your right hand is closed, except for the first finger, which is extended. Tap the back of the left hand with this extended first finger. Turn your left hand over and open it, showing that the coin is gone. Meanwhile, drop your cupped hand to your side.

Say, "Oh, here it is!" Reach into the air with your left hand and apparently grasp a coin, closing the hand. But when you open the hand, no coin is there.

Staring at the empty hand, you're puzzled. "I guess not."

With the left first finger, point upward and to the right. "There it is!" you declare, reaching out with your right hand and producing the coin at your fingertips.

In Your Ear

A gain, with the left hand you reach into the air for a coin, saying, "Here it is!" or "I've got it!"

But, alas, you're wrong. You search the air and then notice Billy. Reaching for his left ear with your right hand, you discover that the coin was there all along.

Slap 1

As usual, in the next two reappearances, the coin is presumed to be in the left hand, but is actually in the right.

Your left hand is closed. Turn the hand palm down. Open it as you slap the palm against the top of your right leg.

At the same time, bring your right hand palm up beneath the leg.

Turn your left hand over, showing that the hand is empty and that no coin rests on the leg. Then bring the palm-up right hand out, showing that the coin has passed through the leg.

Slap 2

As above, your left hand is closed. Open it as you slap it against the left side of the left leg. Promptly slap the right hand against the right side of the right leg, opening the hand and pushing the coin against the leg.

Turn both hands palm outward, showing that the coin has passed through both legs and, in my case, the considerable space between.

Double Cross

The next three or four moves can be combined to form a powerful miniroutine, and any one of them can be performed separately to good effect.

The sleight in *Double Cross* is not difficult, but it does require perfect timing, so a fair amount of practice is necessary.

Hold a large coin between the first and second fingers of your right hand, as shown in Illus. 21. The left hand is held in a palm-down fist.

"This experiment depends upon magic X's," you say. "First, we put X-traordinary X's on my X-cellent X-tremity here." Indicate your left hand. Rapidly move the coin back and forth across the back of the hand, forming an X each time.

Illus. 21

Next, draw the right hand back and up several inches. As you do so, curl in all your fingers, so that the coin can be grasped at the base of the thumb and first finger. Immediately extend all the fingers of the right hand (Illus. 22). In the same motion, make a darting movement toward

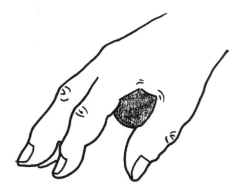

Illus. 22

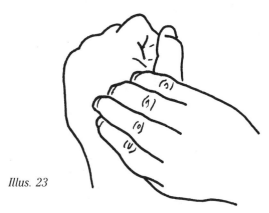

Illus. 23

the left hand, stopping when the tips of the right fingers are gently resting on the back of the left hand (Illus. 23).

You are now going to turn the left hand palm up and lightly draw a few X's across it with the outstretched fingers of the right hand. The first line of the first X will run diagonally, as shown in Illus. 24. But while drawing that first line, a great deal happens:

Illus. 24

(1) The left hand is almost palm up, and you're still turning it. Open the hand slightly. This is completely concealed by the right hand.

(2) As the right hand starts drawing the first line of an X, you let the right thumb relax its grip on the coin, which drops into the palm of the left hand.

(3) Immediately close the left hand again.

(4) You complete the first line of the X. Then you add the other line, and throw in at least two more X's.

While performing this maneuver, say, "And, of course, we must cross the palm a few times."

Next, turn the left hand palm down again and make a few X's with the right fingers across its back. "A few X-tra X's should do it."

With the right hand, make a magical wave at the left hand. Slowly turn the left hand over and show that the coin has penetrated the hand.

Note: The transfer of the coin from the right to the left hand takes only a fraction of a second. Done properly, the entire move is covered by the back of the right hand. Even when the timing is a tad off, plenty of misdirection is provided by the snappy crossing movements.

Coin Toss

This or *More of the Same*, which is the following trick, could be phase two of the miniroutine I mentioned.

The *Coin Toss* requires considerable practice, but the result is that you will have an excellent quick trick for the rest of your life.

A large coin is on the palm of your left hand, fairly near the thumb (Illus. 25). Make a loose fist with the left hand, and then turn it palm down. Show that the right hand is empty. Turn it palm down and place it on top of the left hand (Illus. 26). Note that the thumb, the fingers, and the beginning of the palm rest on the left hand.

Revolve the left hand slightly counterclockwise. At the same time, make a quick upward movement of the two hands, allowing the coin to jump from the left hand and hit against the palm of the right hand. Immediately, the right hand moves forward, as the left hand moves back to its original position. Thus, the coin now rests on the back of the hand.

Without pause, move both hands together in a fast up-and-down motion. Make at least four rapid repetitions. This tends to obscure the original movement. "Sometimes I can actually shake the coin through my hand," you say.

Illus. 25

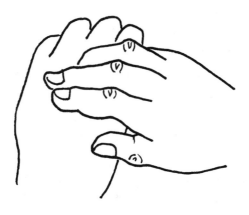

Illus. 26

43

Pause. Then slowly lift the right hand, showing that the coin now rests on top of the left hand.

More of the Same

How about a more elaborate use of the *Coin Toss*?

Show a fairly large coin and explain, "When I flip a coin, I often wonder what hand I should catch it with." Flip the coin and catch it in the palm of your left hand. Close your left hand into a loose fist and turn it palm down. As you continue talking, move the *left* hand up and down a bit so that the coin moves nearer to the thumb. The right side of the left hand now forms a kind of tunnel with the coin resting on the thumb and the first joint of the first and second fingers.

"But what if I had caught the coin with my right hand? I'll tell you what I'd do. I'd slap it right on top of my left hand, like this."

Slap the right hand onto the back of the left as though placing a coin there. Place only the fingers onto the back of the left hand, not the palm. This is relevant to the tricky move you're about to make.

Address Joanie: "Then you'd have to tell me whether the coin is heads or tails. So what do you think it *would* be?"

As you say the word "would," simultaneously move both hands upward several inches and also toward Joanie several inches. The coin comes out of the tunnel formed by the left hand and is placed under the palm of the right hand, which rises slightly to accept the coin. The right hand then moves slightly so that the palm now covers the back of the left hand. And beneath the palm is the coin.

The entire move is done in a fraction of a second and is quite well concealed by the simultaneous move toward the spectator.

Joanie makes her call, and you now use a bit of time misdirection. Let's say that she calls heads. "So Joanie thinks the coin would be heads. Does anyone agree with her?" Get some opinions from others.

"Well, let's take a look." Slowly lift your right hand, showing that the coin now rests on the back of the left hand.

Don't comment on how the coin penetrated the hand. Instead, say something like, "Oh, so it is heads. Good guess, Joanie."

Proceed to your next trick.

Drop Vanish

This move, usually used to make a coin vanish, can provide an excellent climax to the miniroutine. If you are using the move as part of the routine, take the coin from the back of the left hand. Casually toss it back and forth between your hands, ending with it in the left hand.

Hold the coin in the left hand between the fingers and thumb. Display the coin by turning the hand so that the back is to the audience and the fingertips are pointed up (Illus. 27). Make sure there is no space between the fingers.

Turn the right hand so that its back is to the audience and bring it in front of the left. Seemingly you are to grasp

Illus. 27

the coin between the thumb and fingers of the right hand (Illus. 28). Actually, as you apparently grasp the coin, the left hand releases it, letting it drop into the palm of the left hand. Move the right hand away, keeping your eyes on the presumed coin.

Briefly hold the right hand up, apparently displaying the coin just as you did with the left hand. The thumb should be

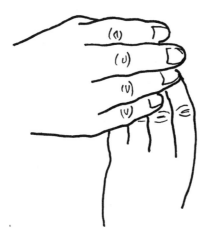

Illus. 28

positioned somewhat lower than in the original position for the left hand. This automatically makes the right-hand fingers straighter and creates the illusion that the coin, although not visible, is actually there. (As a matter of fact, many will think they actually see the coin.)

Form a loose fist with the left hand and turn it palm down. You now have two choices. In the first, you can simply bring the right hand over and apparently push the coin through the back of the hand. That is, you press the right-hand fingers against the back of the hand and then slide them forward an inch or so. Tap the back of the left hand, withdraw the right hand, and show the coin in the left hand. In the second method, you apparently place the coin on the back of the left hand, covering it with the right hand. Duplicate the rapid up-and-down movements of both hands described in the previous sleight, saying, "Maybe if I shake my hands just right, I can get the coin to go the other way." Show that you've been successful.

Notes:

(1) Practice using a mirror. First, actually take the coin, and then perform the sleight. When both moves are identical, you've mastered the sleight.

(2) Make sure the left hand does not move when the coin drops into the palm. There is a tendency to make a slight catching motion; this would be a dead giveaway.

Flip of a Coin

I f you know how to flip a coin into the air and then catch it, the next two tricks may be for you.

Start by balancing a good-sized coin on the nail of your right thumb, resting the side of the coin against the inside of your first finger (Illus. 29). Tell a spectator, "Call heads or tails while the coin is in the air."

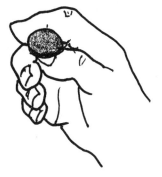

Illus. 29

Move your right thumb upward with a quick motion, causing the coin to spin into the air. The spectator makes his call. You catch the coin in the palm of your right hand.

Make sure that it lands so that one edge rests at the crease formed by the bottom of the fingers (Illus. 30). If the coin is farther back in the palm, jiggle it slightly till it arrives at its proper position.

Illus. 30

Look at the face of the coin as it rests on your palm. If it's the same as what the spectator called, simply turn your right hand over and slap the coin onto the back of your left hand. Lift the hand and show that the spectator was wrong. For example, the spectator calls, "Heads," and the coin lands head-side up. You slap the coin onto the back of your left hand so that the tails side is uppermost.

But suppose the spectator calls,"Heads," and the coin lands on your right hand, showing tails. Clearly, when you slap the coin on your hand in the regular way, the spectator will be proven correct. So, *you don't slap the coin on your hand in the regular way.* Instead, move your right hand forward and cup the fingers while turning it palm down. The result is that the coin naturally turns over as it falls onto your fingers. Immediately slap the coin onto the back of your hand in the regular way. Sure enough, the spectator loses.

You'll be amazed at how quickly you learn the move. Practice the trick move slowly at first. Then work on getting it to look exactly the same as the legitimate move.

The stunt may be repeated any number of times.

Notes:

(1) If you don't wish to perfect the move, here's an alternative. Again, suppose the spectator calls, "Heads." When the coin lands on your hand, tails is showing. Simply hold out your right hand, showing that the spectator is wrong.

Need I say that this version should only be done *once*?

(2) When the coin lands on your right hand, you can't stare at it while making up your mind. You should be able to take a quick glance and then act. This takes a bit of practice.

Part 2

Coin Con

No skill is required for this effective little fooler, but the timing must be perfect. I prefer to use a nickel, although any size coin will do.

Show the coin in the palm of your right hand. Bounce the coin on your hand a few times so that it moves toward the fingers. With your right thumb, move the coin to the fingertips, where you grip it between thumb and fingers (Illus. 31). Note that the coin protrudes a bit beyond the fingers. Hold your right hand up, its back toward the group.

Illus .31

Turn the left hand palm down and make it into a fist. Tell the audience, "With this coin and this fist, I'm going to attempt a feat which some of the greatest magicians in the world are incapable of—I'm going to pass solid through solid."

With your right hand, push the coin against the back of the left hand. Illus. 32 shows the audience view. Withdraw your right hand, still holding the coin, which should be out of view.

Illus. 32

Turn your left hand over and open it. "There you are. The coin has passed right through..." You look puzzled. Look at your left hand in disbelief. Show the coin in your right hand. Toss it onto the open palm of the left hand. Extend the left hand so that all can see the coin there. *"That's* what you were supposed to see when I opened my hand."

Shake your head. "Some of the world's greatest magicians can't do it; I guess that makes me one of the world's greatest magicians."

As you say this, pick up the coin with your right hand. Turn the left hand palm down and make it into a fist. "I'll try one more time."

Push the coin against the back of the left hand. Withdraw the right hand. Turn the left hand over and open it, showing the coin lying on your palm.

You have passed solid through solid!

Oh, I left out a detail. You don't actually pick the coin up

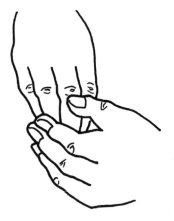

Illus. 33

with your right hand; you leave it in the palm of the left hand. I don't think I've ever seen this move adequately explained. I'll take a shot at it:

Tilt the left hand back toward you slightly while starting to reach toward the left palm (Illus. 33). Spectators see only the backs of your two hands. The right fingers and thumb are separated by about two inches as you reach.

The right hand dips into the left. The fingers are in front of the coin, and the thumb is behind it. The right fingers scrape across the palm toward the right thumb, which remains *motionless*. This movement of the right fingers is what creates the illusion of picking up the coin.

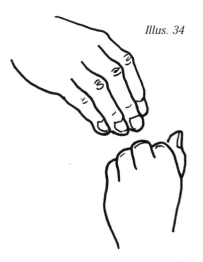

Illus. 34

Illus. 35

As the right hand starts to withdraw, the left hand forms a fist (Illus. 34). The hands move apart. The left hand, now a fist, turns palm down. The right hand is held up, apparently displaying the coin. (Illus. 35 shows your view.) This display is quite brief. It's at this point that you say, "I'll try one more time."

You now duplicate the action you performed as you tried to push the coin through the back of your hand. Withdraw your right hand. For all the spectators know, the coin could still be in the right hand. So, to properly flummox everyone, don't show the right hand immediately.

Instead, say, "Let's see if it worked this time."

Turn your left hand over, open it, and show the coin. Only then, open your right hand, showing that it's empty. Smile and say, "Good!"

Tricky Tumblers

I believe that Martin Gardner gets credit for the basic idea behind *Tricky Tumblers*. I have added the coins and the comedic bit. It is an ideal stunt to introduce a coin trick.

You will need two drinking glasses and two coins. Set the two coins on the table about six inches apart. Behind them set the two glasses, mouth up. Say, "I am now going to com-

Illus. 36

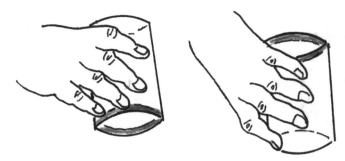

Illus. 37

pletely enclose each coin inside an upside-down glass. Then I am going to cause one of the coins to join the other."

From above, grip the two glasses, the one on the left in the left hand and the one on the right in the right hand. The glass on the left should have your thumb on its left side, and the one on the right should have your thumb on its right side (Illus. 36).

Turn the glasses over simultaneously. Turn the one on the left clockwise and place it, mouth down, on the coin on the left. At the same time, turn the one on the right counterclockwise, but swing it in a full circle so that, at the conclusion, it is once more mouth up as you place it onto the coin on the right (Illus. 37). Quickly remove both hands.

To get laughs, you'll have to do some acting. Look pleased at first, nodding your head. Then gaze at the glasses as your expression changes to puzzlement. Tap the bottom of the glass on the left and stick your fingers into the glass on the right. Pick the glasses up and examine them. Finally, set them down again in their original positions.

Repeat your speech *exactly*: "I am now going to completely enclose each coin inside an upside-down glass. Then I am going to cause one of the coins to join the other." Do the move again. Smile. "There, that's more like it." Notice the glasses. The one on the right is still mouth up. Gradually, you are becoming more exasperated than puzzled.

Repeat the speech and the whole routine, quite a bit faster now. Clearly you are angry when you see the same stupid result. *Now* do the speech and the routine just as fast as possible. At the end, you are fuming and out of breath. But the result is the same.

Lift the glasses off the coins and very deliberately set them aside. "Now," you say with grim determination, "I *am* going to cause one of the coins to join the other." Pick up the coin on the right and toss it on top of the one on the left.

"Let's try something else," you grumble. And you use one or both coins for the next trick.

Good Times

"**I** believe that there's a strong connection between numbers and magic," you explain with your usual veracity. "Let's find out if that's true by conducting a little experiment."

Ask Lily to help out. Since she's a strong believer in numerology, she'll be happy to assist. Hand her two coins of different values. Let's suppose you hand her a one-cent piece (penny) and a ten-cent piece (dime).

Turn your back and tell her, with appropriate pauses:

"Lily, I'd like you to put the penny in one hand and the dime in the other hand. Now, multiply the value of the coin in your left hand by 2, 4, 6, or 8. Then multiply the value of the coin in your right hand by 1, 3, 5, or 7. You should have two results; add these two together, and tell me the total."

Hold this thought: The number one is odd, so the penny or one-cent piece is also odd. The number 10 is even, so the dime or 10-cent piece is also even.

Lily gives you a two-digit number. The digit on the left reveals what she holds in her left hand; the digit on the right reveals what she holds in her right hand. One of the digits will be odd, and the other will be even. The number, for instance, might be 74. The 7 indicates the left hand. It's an odd number, so the penny is in the left hand. The second digit, 4, indicates the right hand. Since it's an even number, the right hand holds the dime.

Another example: Lily says that her total is 43. The digit on the left, 4, is even, so Lily holds the 10-cent piece (even number) in her left hand. And, of course, the penny is in the right.

Note: For the trick to work, one coin must have an odd value and the other an even value. Any two coins that fit this description will do. But we choose the one-cent piece and the ten-cent piece to make it easier for the spectator to perform the math.

What's the Difference?

A s far as I could determine, John Benzais is the inventor of this clever stunt.

In your right pants pocket, there should be (in ascending order of size) a dime, a penny, and a nickel.

Sit down at a table. Tom is good at sitting, so ask him to sit down across from you. Reach into your pocket and separate the nickel from the other two coins, so that it will be somewhat apart from the others when you take them out.

Remove the coins from your pocket. Put your hands under the chair at the sides near the front and hoist yourself forward so that your legs are well under the table.

Remove your hands from the chair and, since they are under the table, bring them above the legs as part of the motion of bringing them out and up. As you do so, deposit the nickel on the outer portion of the right leg, just above the knee.

Bring the other two coins out and toss them onto the table.

"Tom, please check the coins to see if there's anything peculiar about them." Anyone else may examine them as well.

Pick up the coins in your *right* hand. "If it's all right with you, Tom, we'll now try a little experiment."

Start to put your hand under the table. Pause. "I'd like you to put your hand under the table also, Tom. Hold it palm up, please."

As you're saying this, you leave the dime on your leg and pick up the nickel. Reach your hand farther under the table and drop the nickel and the penny onto Tom's open palm.

Leave your hand under the table. "Without looking at the coins, Tom, I'd like you to hand me the penny."

Tom will undoubtedly feel the difference in size of the two coins and hand you the nickel. You leave the nickel on your leg and pick up the dime. Then bring your hand out, holding the dime in your fist.

"Tom, please close your hand into a fist and bring the coin out." He does so.

"You hold the dime, and I hold the penny, right?" Don't wait for an answer. "Let's touch fists." You tap his fist with yours.

"Let's open up now." You both open your hands. He holds the penny, and you hold the dime.

"I make more darned money that way."

While saying this, toss the dime into your left hand and let your right hand fall naturally into your lap.

Look into Tom's eyes. "Could I have my penny back, please."

Move your left hand forward, indicating that Tom should put the penny with the dime. As Tom puts the coin into your left hand, your right hand picks up the nickel from your leg. Bring the left hand a little below the table and toss the two coins into the slightly cupped right hand. Shake the coins as though shaking dice, and then return all three to the right pants pocket.

Note: Without realizing it, I once chose a wisenheimer to assist me with this trick. Instead of handing me the nickel, he gave me the penny. Thus, I ended up with a dime, and he had a nickel. Presumably, a nickel was never involved.

After we touched fists and opened our hands, I said, "So I now have the dime which you held, and I have magically changed your penny into a nickel."

I got rid of the coins as fast I could, and moved on.

It has never happened to me, but I suppose someone could bring out the two coins and look at them. If that should occur, I would probably say, "Look at that. The magic has happened already," and quickly get rid of all the coins.

Lost Money

H ere is an old trick to which I have added some byplay and a strong conclusion.

You will need two large coins of the same value. A bit of preparation is also necessary, but this can be done quite casually while chatting with the group or while the group's attention is directed elsewhere. Secretly grip one of the coins in your right hand, holding it between the thumb and second finger so that the flat side is parallel to the floor. Hold the second coin in front of, and perpendicular to, the other. Illus. 38 shows how the coins are positioned. It's show time!

Illus. 38

Illus. 39

Display the front coin at about shoulder level (Illus. 39). (The other coin will be completely hidden.) If some spectators are seated and others are standing, lower your hand about six inches. As you show the coin, you may revolve it clockwise and counterclockwise, but do not tip it forward or back.

"A peculiar coin!" declare to the audience. You will need an assistant. "Jay, I wonder if you'd help me in a little guessing game. Just watch the coin."

Hold your left hand out in a cupped position just below the right hand. Dip the right hand into the left palm (Illus. 40). Drop the front coin into the left hand. Instantly close the right hand into a fist, enclosing the hidden coin. Remove the right fist from the left hand, which is still cupped.

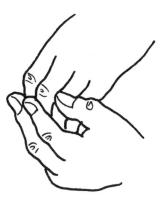

Illus. 40

Form the left hand into a fist, enclosing its coin. Each hand now holds a coin. As far as the spectators know, however, it's only one hand that holds a coin. And they cannot tell which one it is.

"Watch carefully, Jay."

Both fists are held palm down (Illus. 41). Rapidly cross your hands, passing the right hand over the left. Return the hands to their original positions. Again, cross your hands, this time passing the right hand *under* the left. The hands

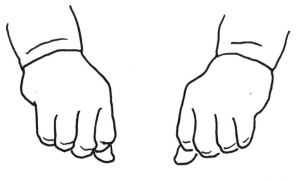

Illus. 41

return to their original positions. Perform the original crossing maneuver once more. All of this should be done quite rapidly and without pausing.

Turn both fists palm up. Perform the exact same crossing maneuvers. Turn both hands palm down. They should be at least six inches apart. "All right, Jay. Which hand holds the coin?" Whichever he names, open the other hand to show that he is wrong. "Sorry, Jay. You'll have to watch more closely." Close the hand and turn it palm down. You are now ready to repeat the stunt.

You may do this trick three or four times. Finally, when Jay chooses, open the *selected* hand to show that he is correct. "Good choice, Jay! This must be your lucky day. As a matter of fact, you couldn't miss." Open the other hand to show the coin there. You end up with both hands held out palms up and a coin in the middle of each.

Note: Throughout the trick, make sure you keep each hand tightly closed so that no one gets a peek at the coin within.

Free Choice

A re you familiar with the "magician's choice?" The magician has three objects and wants to force the spectator to choose a particular one. A good example can be found in This Is Your Choice.

Subir Kumar Dhas developed an excellent example with coins. For his trick, you'll need two coins—one large and one small. In the United States, these would be a 50-cent piece and a 5-cent piece. Furthermore, reference will be made to a coin of intermediate value—a 25-cent piece, for instance.

The 50-cent piece and the 5-cent piece are in your right pants pocket.

Start by taking from your pocket the 50-cent and the 5-cent pieces. Arrange it so that when your hand emerges from the pocket, the 50-cent piece is on top of the 5-cent piece and you're holding the 50-cent piece with your thumb

Illus. 42

Illus. 43

(Illus. 42). Don't let anyone see the coins, however. Hold your hand up so that all can see its back (Illus. 43). Announce, "In this hand, I have my prediction."

Move your right hand close to your chest, making it impossible for anyone to see what you're holding.

Ask Stewart to help you out. Hold out your *left* hand, open and palm up. Say to Stewart, "I'd like you to visualize three coins lying in my hand: a 50-cent piece, a 25-cent piece, and a 5-cent piece. Please concentrate, Stewart, and choose one of the three coins." Pause. "Have you done it? Which one did you pick?"

If he names the 50-cent piece, do the following: Lower your right hand, showing that you're holding that coin (with the 5-cent piece hidden beneath it). Lift up your right thumb so that all can see the coin clearly (Illus. 44). (Warning: Lift up the thumb and move it to the right, but make sure that you do not move your fingers; you don't want the top coin to slide, thus revealing the coin beneath it, either by sound or sight.)

Say to Stewart, "I knew you'd choose the 50-cent piece." Place your thumb back on top of the 50-cent piece and return the coins to your pocket. Make sure there's no give-away "clink" while depositing the coins there.

Illus. 44

If he names the 5-cent piece, do the following: Say, "All right, Stewart, now please choose one of the other two coins—the 50-cent piece or the 25-cent piece."

If he names the 25-cent piece, you say, "So you've chosen the 5-cent piece and the 25-cent piece, leaving me with what?" He naturally names the 50-cent piece. "Right," you say, and show the 50-cent piece exactly as described above.

But suppose he has named the 5-cent piece and, when asked to name one of the other coins, says, "The 50-cent piece." Tell Stewart, "You have chosen the 5-cent piece and the 50-cent piece." Close your right hand into a loose fist. Bring it forward, and then shake it so that the coins rattle. Open your hand, showing both coins. "And here they are."

If he names the 25-cent piece, say: "I can't believe it, Stewart. You removed the 25-cent piece and left me with the other two coins. I was hoping you'd do that." Show the two coins as described immediately above.

Note that every step seems perfectly natural. Be sure to practice until the different steps are virtually automatic.

Rubber Money

How about an amusing stunt? Suppose you've been performing a number of tricks with a large coin—let's say a 50-cent piece.

Explain, "If you'd been paying close attention, you'd have noticed how I was able to perform these various feats. Nothing to it at all, *if* you use a rubber coin."

Hold the coin at opposite edges with the tips of the fingers and the thumb of both hands (Illus. 45). Move the fin-

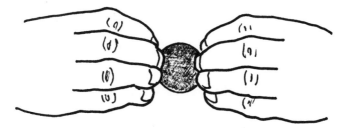

Illus. 45

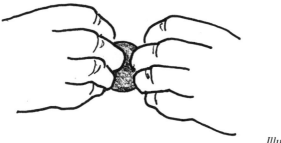

Illus. 46

gers of both hands *inward* and the thumbs *outward*, as though bending the coin so that the edges are moving forward and the middle backward (Illus. 46). At the same time, enhance the illusion by moving both hands backward an inch or so.

Return your fingers to their original positions, remembering to move the hands forward an inch or so. Apparently, you are bending the coin back and forth.

Repeat this movement quite rapidly several times. The illusion is that the coin is indeed rubbery.

Note: You should probably perform this stunt standing up. For some reason, I find that I can do the bending motions much more rapidly and *convincingly* when I'm standing.

Folding Money

A Fool and His Money

As far as I know, Don Tabor developed this trick using silken handkerchiefs. Don Nielsen came up with the version that uses bills.

I use a five-dollar bill and a one-dollar bill, but any two bills of different denominations will do.

"They say that a fool and his money are soon parted. So, while I'm doing this stunt, I'm going to keep a close eye on my money."

Display the two bills. "Here I have a one-dollar bill and a five-dollar bill. Let's wind them up."

Fold the one-dollar bill in half lengthwise. Give it a sharp crease by running your first finger and thumb over the fold. Then fold it in half lengthwise again, once more creasing it. Do the same with the five-dollar bill. (In following the illustrations, notice that, for clarity, both folded bills are shown as much thinner than they actually are. And the five-dollar bill is shaded, also for clarity.)

Hold the one-dollar bill straight up. Place the five-dollar bill in front of it as shown in Illus. 47. Fold the right side of the five-dollar bill down and behind the one-dollar bill (Illus.

48). Fold the bottom portion of the five up and across the front of the one (Illus. 49). Take the bottom of the one and fold it back and up, behind the point where the bills intersect (Illus. 50). Bring this same end over and in front of the intersection (Illus. 51).

"Now, they are not just wound up—they are locked

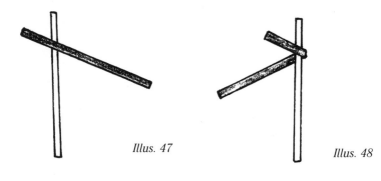

Illus. 47

Illus. 48

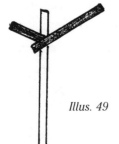

Illus. 49

Illus. 50

Illus. 51

together." Have a spectator take the two ends of the five. You take the two ends of the one. "Let's pull and wiggle," you urge. The spectator and you should jockey the bills up and down and side to side. Eventually, they separate.

"I may or may not be a fool," you declare, "but I can tell you this: My money soon parted!"

A Wad of Money

The only preparation for this trick is to take a dollar bill, wad it up, and stick it into a convenient pocket.

Begin by displaying a newspaper page. Tear two small strips from it, each approximately the size of the bill that has been wadded up. Ask two spectators to help out. Give one of the strips to each of them.

"Please wad these up." As they do this, casually stick your right hand into your pocket. Grip the wadded bill so that it is held by the third and fourth fingers. (This is actually the *Finger Palm*, page 16. The difference is that here the object is held between the third and fourth fingers, rather than the second and third.) When you bring the hand from the pocket, cup it slightly, keeping the bill concealed (Illus. 52).

"Would you each place the wad on the palm of your

hand." They do so. "Now, we have to choose one." Let them decide which one to use.

"Excellent choice," you declare as you pick up the selected wad between the thumb and the first two fingers of the right hand. You should hold it as shown in Illus. 53.

Apparently, you now drop the wad of newspaper into

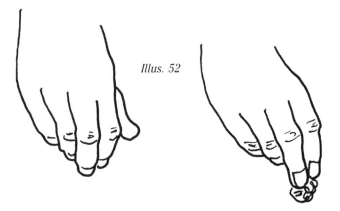

Illus. 52

Illus. 53

your left hand. Instead, you drop the wadded bill. Here's how: Hold the cupped left hand palm up. Bring the right hand palm down above the left hand (Illus. 54). Retain your grip on the wadded newspaper and release the wadded bill. Briefly display the wadded bill on the palm of your left hand and then close your fingers over it. Meanwhile, let the cupped right hand drop to your side. As you do this, let the wad move back in the right hand so that it can be gripped with the third and fourth fingers. This is the same grip as that used when removing the bill from your pocket.

Still holding your left hand up, reach out with the right

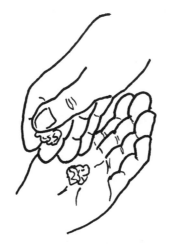

Illus. 54

hand and take the other wadded newspaper strip between the right thumb and first two fingers. "You did not choose this one." Place the newspaper wad in your pocket, leaving the other one there as well.

While you place the wads in your pocket, continue your patter: "When I was a child, my father wanted me to sell newspapers. He said to me, 'There's real money in newspapers.'" While saying this, hold up your left hand. "Let's see if he's right." Hand the wad to one of the spectators and ask him to open it up. "Now, hold it up so everyone can see it. See? A word of warning: Do not try this at home; it won't work."

Presidential Headstand

You can perform this either sitting at a table or standing up.

Hold a dollar bill between your two hands, so that others can see that George Washington is upside down.

"There's George standing on his head. How ridiculous! How unpresidential!"

Fold the top half of the bill down and forward (away

Illus. 55

Illus. 56

Illus. 57

from you), as shown in Illus. 55. Then fold the right half of the bill forward (Illus. 56). You are holding the reduced bill at its ends. Again, fold the right half of the bill forward. Both ends of the bill are nearest you on the left side.

Now, grip the nearest end with your right hand and turn it to the right, as though opening the back cover of a book. Grip the other end with your left hand and pull that portion to the left. You are now holding the bill folded in half as shown in Illus. 57. Reach over with the right hand and raise the front half. The spectators now see Washington right-side up.

"That's more like it. We've had enough presidents who didn't know which way was up."

A Roll of Bills
·····························

All you need for this trick are two bills of different denominations, perhaps a five and a one. Place the five flat on the table and the one on top of it, so that the bottom half-inch of the five shows (Illus. 58). As you place each bill down, call attention to its value.

Starting at the bottom, carefully roll up the two bills. As you reach the halfway point, ask Darlene, "Which one would you prefer, the bill on the bottom or the bill on top?"

She will undoubtedly prefer the one on the bottom. As you continue rolling the bills, say, "Personally, I would much prefer the bill on top."

When you have almost completely rolled the bills, let one end flip over, and then stop. The end that flips over is that of the five-dollar bill. Hold this down with the left first finger while unrolling the two bills. The five-dollar bill is now on top.

Illus. 58

Point to the five. "Definitely, I prefer the bill on top."

Repeat the stunt, asking for Darlene's choice when you reach the midpoint in the rolling. She is wrong again, for you always control the result. If you want the bill underneath to come out on top, you let one end flip over. If you want the bills to remain in the same order, you let both ends flip over. Don't forget to place your left first finger on the upper edge of the last bill that flipped over before you unroll the two bills.

You may increase the fun by having one spectator succeed every time while another always fails. After several alternating turns, you might explain, "Well, some people are good with money, and some people aren't."

It's An Ill Wind

Take any bill and fold it in the middle so that one side touches the other. Set it on the table, so that it resembles a miniature tent (Illus. 59).

Illus. 59

Lean over the table as you rub the first finger of your right hand against your sleeve. Then point the first finger at the bill as though you're pointing a gun (Illus. 60).

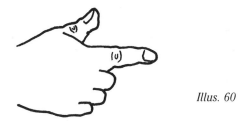

Illus. 60

Wiggle your thumb and quickly move your hand up a bit, as though firing your digital weapon. And the little tent falls over!

How did you do it, you little miracle-worker? Actually, there's nothing to it. At the exact moment that you fired your "weapon," you opened your lips slightly and ever so lightly blew on the bill's lower edge.

Actually, I lied a little. There is something to it. You'd better practice so that you can synchronize the "shot" and the blowing perfectly. Also, you need to determine exactly how hard you must blow.

Dice

Countless puzzling tricks can be performed with dice. And for many of them, no special skill is required. In fact, only one of the following dice tricks calls for sleight of hand. But this does not mean that the other tricks are inferior. As a matter of fact, they're quite baffling and magical.

Triple the Fun

Chet can put two and two together, so you might ask him to help out.

Place three dice on the table and turn away. "Chet, I'd like you to roll all three dice until you're satisfied with the numbers you get."

This, of course, is to make sure everyone knows that the dice are normal in every way.

Continue, with appropriate pauses: "Chet, quietly add up the numbers on the faces. Pick up one die and turn it over so that you can see the number on the bottom. Add this number to your total. Finally, roll that same die and add the number on its face to the total."

You turn back to the group, saying, "There's no way in

the world I can know which die you decided to roll again, right?"

Then, while casually picking up the dice, announce the total that Chet came up with.

You're right, of course. You simply added up the numbers showing on the faces and then added seven.

The method is quite easy, but the procedure throws spectators off.

The opposite sides of a die always total seven. And here's how Chet reaches his total: The two dice that he does not pick up are added together, and the resulting total is available to the performer. Chet picks up one die. He has already added the top side to the total; he now adds the bottom side. In other words, he adds seven to the total.

Thus far, we have the total of the two dice that are not picked up, plus seven. Chet rolls the die that he picked up. The number on the face of this die, which is added to the total, is also available to the performer. So he simply adds seven to the total showing and gets the correct answer.

The Hidden Numbers

A s long as you have the three dice, you might as well astonish Chet again. Place the dice back on the table.

Turn away, saying, "Chet, I'd like you to throw the dice several times, and then pile them very neatly, one on top of the other."

When he's done, turn back and take a *quick* casual look at the pile (Illus. 61). After that, make it a point to keep your eyes off the pile of dice.

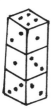

Illus. 61

"Chet, there are *five* hidden numbers in that pile of dice. No one can possibly see those numbers without removing the dice from the pile, right?"

As usual, you're right.

"In fact, from where each of us stands, we can only see some of the *visible* numbers. And I'd like you to note that I'm not even looking at those. Nevertheless, I'm going to try to guess what that total might be."

Concentrate for a moment while staring off into space. Then name a total.

"Now, let's add up those hidden numbers. Lift off the top die, Chet, and look at the number on the bottom. What is it?" He announces it. Suppose he says 3.

"Good. Set that die aside. Now, what number are you looking at? Let's say that it's 5.

"Five. Five and three is eight. So far, we have eight. What's the next hidden number—the one on the bottom of that die?"

In this instance, Chet will say 2. "So we add the two to eight, and we now have 10. Please set that die aside."

Continue by adding the top and bottom of the last die. Make sure you go slowly enough so that everyone can see that the addition is correct.

In our example, the total will be 17. And this is the number you announced.

You did such a good job of acting that no one realizes how simple the trick really is. When you took that sneaky glance at the dice, you noted the number showing on top of the pile, and subtracted this from 21. This reveals the total of the hidden numbers. The top die in our example showed 4. You subtracted this from 21, getting 17.

Earlier I mentioned that opposite sides of a die always total 7. You had Chet add up the opposite sides of all the dice except the top one. He added only the bottom of this die; therefore, the total of all the hidden numbers will be 21 minus the value showing on the face of the top die.

Stack the Dice

F or this trick, which was developed by Martin Gardner, we'll give Chet a rest and ask Jane to help out.

Pick up one of the dice so that only two are on the table.

Provide Jane with these directions, pausing at the proper places:

(1) "Please roll the dice until you're satisfied with the numbers on top."

(2) "Put one die on top of the other."

(3) "Note the number showing on top. That's your first number."

(4) "Pick up that top die. Turn it over so that you can see the number on the bottom. Add that to your first number."

(5) "Look at the number showing on the die on the table. Add that to your total."

(6) "Add four to your total."

(7) "Roll the die that you're holding, and add the number showing on top."

(8) "Slide the two dice so that they're next to each other. Turn them over so that you're looking at the opposite sides. Add these two numbers to your total."

Again, this trick is based on the idea that opposite sides of a die always total 7. Gardner, a most inventive magician and mathematical wizard, worked out a method in which this principle is well hidden. The final total will always be 21, unless you toss in an additional number as I did with step 6 above. Since I added four to the total, the final number will be 21 + 4, or 25. You, of course, can throw in whatever number you wish for step 6.

But how do we arrive at 21? Consider that one of the dice is A, and the other is B. In steps 3 and 4, you add together the top and bottom of die A, and you pick up the die. Thus far, you have seven.

In step 5, you add in the *top side* of die B.

In step 7, you roll die A and add the *top side*.

In step 8, you add the *bottom sides* of both die A and die B. This means that in steps 5, 7, and 8 you have added 14 to the total. You already had 7, so 14 + 7 = 21.

Not a Fair Shake

Here's an unusual game played with dice. Since Zeke is a fairly good loser, he'll be the perfect victim.

Give Zeke a die, and you keep one for yourself.

Explain: "Zeke, we'll take turns showing a number on our die. Each time a number is shown, it's added to the previous total. The winner is the person who reaches *exactly* 50. It can't be *more than* 50; it has to be 50 exactly."

There's no point in telling Zeke the rest of the story—that you'll win every time *if* you start first. And the odds are that you'll win even if he starts first.

Here are the critical numbers: 1, 8, 15, 22, 29, 36, 43. Each time you show your die, the total must add up to one of these numbers. Note that after the first number, each one is a multiple of 7, plus 1.

So, if you start, always begin with the number 1. Thus, Zeke cannot reach the second critical number, 8. Let's say that he shows a 4, bringing the total to 5. You show a 3, bringing the total to 8, the next key number. Whatever he shows from now on, you make sure that your die will bring the total to the next key number.

Another way of putting it is this: Once you hit a total of 8, make sure that Zeke's die and your die total 7. Suppose you've hit 8. Zeke shows a 4; you show a 3. The total of both dice is 7, and you've brought the overall total to the next key number, 15.

The game may be repeated. Your demeanor in choosing numbers is quite important. Pretend that any number will do. Roll the die around in your hand as though whatever number comes up will be just fine.

If Zeke insists that *he* start the game, try to hit a key number as soon as possible. Unless Zeke is unusually bright or actually knows the game (quite unlikely), you should succeed.

Roll 'em

Wonderfully waggish Wally Wilson taught me this remarkable dice trick. It depends upon a secret move that is extremely easy to perform.

First, let me explain an older trick that can be done in combination with the one Wally showed me. Place a pair of dice between the first finger and thumb of the right hand. In Illus. 62, a five and a four are being shown. If you were to revolve your hand clockwise, you'd show a two and a three (Illus. 63). But what if, as you revolve your hand, you also revolve the dice on your thumb by pushing the first finger back. In our example, you'd now be showing a four and a one.

The trick? Show the front of the dice, and name the two numbers. You then revolve your hand clockwise, *also revolving the dice*. Announce the two numbers that now show. Revolve your hand counterclockwise, and at the same time revolve the dice back to their original position.

Repeat the entire procedure.

Ask, "So what two numbers are on the other side?" The group names the two numbers that seem to be on the other side. But when you slowly revolve your hand clockwise and show the two numbers, it turns out that they are quite mis-

Illus. 62

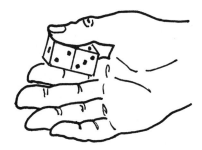

Illus. 63

91

taken. In our example, you'd say, "No, here we have a four and a one."

The hand should be turned fairly rapidly. A bit of practice should make the tricky move impossible to detect. One thing to beware of: It's possible to end up with the same numbers you had when you revolved the dice, so after you grip the dice, secretly check out all three sets of numbers you're going to show.

Now, for the main event! The move involved is quite similar to that used in the first trick.

First, set the two dice onto the table. Turn one of them so that the four is on top (Illus. 64). Keeping the four on top, revolve the die clockwise until a two is below the four when you look at it (Illus. 65).

Pick up the die with the left hand and place it in the right

Illus. 64   *Illus. 65*

hand so that it is held on one side between the tips of the second and third fingers and on the other by the thumb. As shown in Illus. 66, the side with the four on it is being dis-

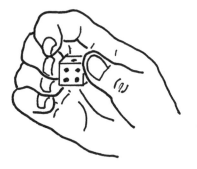

Illus. 66

played. Also, your thumb should be partially covering the two.

Turn the other die so that the two is on top (Illus. 67). Retaining the position of the two, revolve the die clockwise

Illus. 67   *Illus. 68*

until a four is below the two as you look at the die (Illus. 68).

Pick up the die with the left hand and place it on top of the die in the right hand so that it is held on one side

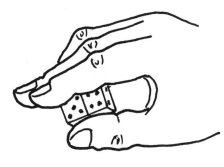

Illus. 69

between the tips of the first and second fingers and on the other by the thumb (Illus. 69). The two is being displayed, and the thumb is partially covering the four.

The thumb is held at the point where the two dice touch, and the dice are almost a half inch back from the ends of the fingers.

This arrangement of the dice isn't done in secret, so it's important that you seem to be simply selecting an appropriate number to display. For instance, while turning the die at the beginning, you might comment, "Let's see, I need a good number to show you." A four faces the front. "No, I'm not sure if that's a good one. I'll find a better one." You say this as you're revolving the die to find the two.

Finally the two shows up. "Good enough. I guess a four

will be all right." Pick up the die with your left hand and place it in the right, as described above.

Do a similar monologue as you turn the other die with your left hand. When you finally have it arranged properly, place it on top of the other die in the right hand.

The spectators are now shown two dice. The one on top displays a two; the one on the bottom displays a four.

Give Marie a good look at the two dice. "I'd like to test your memory, Marie. Here we have two dice. Do you notice what number is on top?" She does. It's a two.

"And the number on the bottom?"

It's a four.

You rapidly move your right hand up and down several times. The length of the perpendicular movement should be about four inches. The speed of the moves increases. When

Illus. 70

you reach maximum speed, *revolve the dice by pushing your thumb forward and moving the middle fingers back.* Perform two or three more up-and-down moves, gradually slowing. Hold the dice so that Marie can see them clearly. Apparently, the top die has changed places with the bottom die (Illus. 70).

"I think you forgot, Marie. The *four* is on top, and the *two* is on the bottom." Pause. "So what do we have?" She tells you.

Perform the up-and-down moves. After the first move, revolve the dice back. This time, of course, you *move the thumb back and the two middle fingers forward.*

Show Marie the dice. "Oh, Marie, your memory is slipping. Didn't we agree that the *two* is on top and the *four* on the bottom?"

You can do it a few more times if you wish. But the trick is probably best done as a quick interlude between other tricks, so two or three times should be plenty.

Notes:

(1) In the example, I've used the numbers four and two. Actually, *you can use any* combination that doesn't add to seven. Five and one, for instance, make a nice contrast.

(2) Instead of arranging the dice on the table, you may prefer to make the arrangement while holding the two dice in the display position (one on top of the other) in the right

hand. This also can work well.

(3)   You've noted that I prefer to hold the two dice between the middle fingers and thumb. This makes it easier for me to revolve the dice. Some performers, however, prefer to hold the dice between the first two fingers and the thumb. You might want to try both ways to see which suits you.

(4)   You might prefer to make a snappier trick like this: Show the dice one on top of the other. Say, "The four's on top and the two's on the bottom. I hope they stay that way."

Perform the move.

Address the dice, "That's not fair. You're supposed to be the other way."

Perform the move. "That's more like it."

Call it quits.

Playing Cards

A Real Magic Spell

Why don't we lead off this category with what I consider the best of the batch, an astonishing trick developed by Dave Altman, who graciously granted permission to include it here? The basic plot is as good as any I've ever seen in magic.

It's essential that the spectator should use between eight and 16 cards. Dave's method of making this happen is extremely clever, as you're about to see.

"For this next experiment, we'll need someone with an excellent imagination," you explain.

If Karl doesn't volunteer, you might just choose him anyway; he has a *really* good sense of humor.

Hand him the deck of cards. "Please give the deck a good shuffle, Karl. While you're doing this, I'd like you to think of the deck as a copy of an adventure novel."

When he finishes shuffling, have him set the deck onto the table. "Please cut off about half the deck and set it down." He does. "We'll make this a *short* novel. Just push one of those piles to one side."

He does. "Now, cut off about half of that other pile and

set it down." He does. "Let's make this a short story, Karl. Please push one of those two piles aside."

In front of him, Karl now has a pile that should consist of between eight and 16 cards. Apparently, you pay no attention to any of the piles, but you should sneak a peek at Karl's final pile. If it looks a little too fat, you might say, "Karl, I think we should have an even shorter story. You'd better take several cards from your pile and set them aside. I'll turn my head away while you're doing it."

Chances are that the cuts have ensured that the number is between eight and 16, so you can proceed.

"You're the hero of this story, Karl. And it just so happens that you're a sorcerer. To start, why don't you choose one card from your packet and put it face up onto the table so we can all see it."

Suppose it's the nine of clubs.

"Now use your imagination, Karl. Think of a female person that you really like, but aren't sure that the feeling is returned. This card, the nine of clubs, will represent that person, who is also in our story. For purposes of the story, let's give her a truly romantic name. We'll call her...Ethel Gertrude." Pause for a laugh.

But don't wait too long.

"Turn Ethel Gertrude face down and then put the rest of your packet face down on top of her. The rest of that packet represents a gang who want to kidnap your heroine. Obviously, they know exactly where she is—at the bottom of the heap. No offense.

"Your job is to hide her so that no one will know where she is. Since you're a sorcerer, maybe you should try a real magic spell." Pause. "Go ahead." Pause for just a second or two. Laugh apologetically, and say, "I'm sorry, just spell out the words, 'a real magic spell.' Take one card off the top of your pile and put it on the bottom for every letter in the spelling."

Make sure that Karl does this correctly.

"Perfect! Now, the kidnappers will never find her. But there's still an important question to be answered. First, we need the magic laying on of hands."

Have him put the packet face down onto the table. Put your right hand flat on the packet. Have him put his right hand on top of yours. Put your left hand on top of his. He puts his left hand on top of all. You say, "Okay, break it up, break it up!" And you both withdraw your hands.

"Pick up the packet and we'll find out whether your dream girl loves you or not. Take a card from the top and put it on the bottom. As you do this, say, 'She loves me.'"

He does it.

"Now, take a card from the top and put it on the table, saying, 'She loves me not.'"

He obliges.

You direct him to transfer the top card to the bottom, saying, "She loves me." Then he takes the top card and places it on top of the one on the table, saying, "She loves me not."

Karl continues until he holds only one card. Don't let him turn it over for a moment.

"Your dream girl is represented by the nine of clubs. If this is the nine of clubs, it means that she's grateful that you saved her, that she returns your love, and that you'll live happily ever after. If not, it means that your life is ruined forever."

He turns the card over. It's the one he chose, all right.

Notes:

(1) The trick will work with "a real magic spell" or any other 15-letter combination.

(2) Why do the hands have to be placed on the cards? If you don't touch the cards in some way, the spectators may well assume that the trick is completely automatic. Which, of course, it is.

(3) The trick can be worked with a woman. She is a sorcerer; her dream man is in danger of being kidnapped. The only real addition is to make up a goofy name for her dream man. I'll pass on that; I'm probably in enough trouble with my choice of Ethel Gertrude.

Sappy Speller

J ohn Bragoli invented a clever comedy spelling trick. I have added somewhat to the trick and thrown in a novelty ending.

In whatever sneaky way you can, get a peek at the bottom card. Then announce to the group, "I am about to perform the world's best card experiment. With no help whatever, I will locate the card that virtually no magician in the world is capable of locating." Suppose the card you peeked at was the four of diamonds. "I refer, of course, to the four of diamonds. And I, with my supereducated fingers, will accomplish this miraculous feat."

As you speak, give the cards an overhand shuffle, shuffling the last several cards individually so that the four of diamonds ends up on top. "To start things rolling, I will cut the deck precisely in half."

Cut off somewhat less or more than half the deck. Count aloud as you deal the cards into a pile on the table. Suppose you have 23 cards. "There we are. Not only have I cut off precisely half the deck, 26 cards... but I have magically caused *three* of those cards to move to the other pile." Slight bow. "Thank you so much."

Pick up the pile of 23 cards that you just dealt onto the

table.

"It's time now to locate the four of diamonds. We have 23 cards. We add the digits... two plus three, giving us five."

From the packet of 23 cards, deal five cards into a pile.

Tap the last card you dealt, saying, "Four of diamonds."

Pause a moment and then turn the card over. "Ah, the six of hearts. Yet another miracle. Not only have I located the four of diamonds, but I also have—in my own mystical way—changed it to the six of hearts. Thank you so much."

Take a small bow.

Turn the face-up card face down. Drop the cards in your hand on top of the packet. Place the entire packet on top of the balance of the deck. The chosen card is now 18th from the top.

"So now...with a few magical words... and a riffle of the deck, we turn the four of diamonds face up in the middle of the deck." Riffle the ends of the deck. Say, "Hocus-pocus, abracadabra."

Rapidly spread through the cards. It's obvious that no card is face up. "There we are... the four of diamonds is face down once more. I turned it face up with 'hocus-pocus'... and, of course, 'abracadabra' turned it face down again." Weak laugh. "Too much of a good thing, I guess."

Since the card is 18th from the top, you could now spell out something in 18 letters to arrive at the card. I decided to try something different. It turned out to be very effective and quite in the spirit of the rest of Mr. Bragoli's trick. You suddenly turn solemn. Turn to the crowd. "I know what you're thinking. This isn't working at all. He can't find the four of diamonds. The so-called experiment really stinks. Well, let me tell you something: *I won't give up. I know I can find that dumb card. Where in the world is it?*" As you speak, you rapidly deal cards into a pile, one card for each syllable uttered. Your intensity increases as you deal the cards. In fact, you end up panting. Pause. Flip over the last card dealt and say casually, "Oh, there it is... the four of diamonds." Lengthy pause. "Yet another miracle!"

Note: Clearly, you may use any words to locate the card. Just make sure there are 18 syllables, and that you deal one card for each syllable. You could, for example, try this:

"I'm exhausted. There's nothing else to try. What a stupid experiment!"

Eighteen syllables here—just remember to deal out one card for each one.

It's All in the Mind

Bob Hummer, an eccentric who was devoted to developing clever magical principles, invented this trick. The original version seemed a trifle obvious, so I threw in a little misdirection.

Ask Abe, who seems fairly honest, to help out. Hand him the deck, saying, "I'd like you to shuffle the deck, Abe."

When he finishes, turn your back. "Please count off seven cards and set the rest of the deck aside."

When he's ready, say, "Look over the seven cards and see if there's one that you really like. Place that one on top of your pile." Pause. "Now, to help me visualize the card, move from the top to the bottom of your pile a number of cards equal to the value of your card. For instance, if your card were a 5, you'd move five cards to the bottom of your pile—one at a time. If your card is a face card, just move... oh, let's say three cards from the top to the bottom. And consider an ace to be a one."

When Abe finishes, turn around and take the cards from him. Hold them face down. "These are kind of hard to shuffle, so I'll just mix them a little."

You now perform a pseudo-shuffle that I developed and named "One-Two-Three Shift." The exact order of the cards is retained, though it appears you are apparently mixing them. In this instance, you're going to transfer 14 cards from the top of the pile to the bottom, thus returning the 7-card pile to its original order. (You could transfer just 7 cards, but this wouldn't be too deceptive.) You transfer the cards one, two, or three at a time.

Let's do it this way. Fan off two cards and place them on the bottom, mentally saying, "Two." Place one card on the bottom, adding the one to the two. So you think, "Three."

Transfer two to the bottom, thinking, "Plus two equals five."

Move one to the bottom, thinking, "Plus one equals six."

Move three to the bottom, thinking, "Plus three equals nine."

Move three more to the bottom, thinking, "Plus three equals twelve."

Move two to the bottom, thinking, "Plus two equals fourteen."

Stop! Fourteen was the number we wanted. If you should happen to overshoot, which is unlikely, you could go right on to 21—or any other multiple of seven.

While this description is pretty labored, the actual shuffle is casual and, apparently, uncalculated.

After performing the One-Two-Three Shift, hand the cards back to Abe. "Please concentrate on your card, Abe." Pause. "Fan them in front of me so that I can see the faces. That might help."

It certainly *will* help. He fans out the cards. You note the value of the card on the face of the packet, mentally saying, "One." If that card happens to be an ace, that may well be Abe's card. But we must check further.

Say *two* to yourself while looking at the card above it. Say *three* while looking at the next card. Continue to the back card of the packet, at which point you mentally say *seven*. Look again at the card at the face of the packet, saying *eight*. Continue through the next two cards, saying *nine* and then *ten*. If only one value matched up with the number you were mentally saying, you're very lucky; and, of course, that one would be the chosen card. Concentrate and tell him the name of his mental selection. For instance, you mentally said six and the card at that point was the six of spades. Clearly, that must be his card.

But what if two or more cards match? If this is the case, you must use a process of elimination. Let's suppose that *three cards* are possible. If two of them are red and one is black, you'd say, "I'm not sure, but I think your card is red." If he says no, you know that it's the black card. If he says yes, then you must perform another elimination. Depending on the values of the two cards, you can guess that it's a low card or an even card. Or you might guess the exact suit. In any instance, you'll never make more than one incorrect guess.

When you count *three* and you see a three there, obviously that could be the chosen card. But don't forget that a face card at the third position might also be the selected one.

Sucker Selections

Many years ago, I adapted a clever principle to a coin trick. Later, I realized that even better use could be made of the same idea in a "sucker" card trick.

Start fanning through the deck without letting the spectators see the faces of the cards. When you come to a black face card—let's say the queen of spades—place it face down on the table. Fan once more through the cards, this time removing all the spot cards of one *red* suit, plus the ace. Place these, one at a time, face down on the queen of spades. Let's say that you remove all the diamonds except the jack, queen, and king. You now have a pile of eleven cards on the table.

Eunice enjoys a good card trick, so invite her to assist you. While chatting with Eunice, casually give the 11-card packet four overhand shuffles. In doing so, it's easy to shuffle the bottom card to the top and then back to the bottom, and then repeat this. If you can't do the overhand shuffle, simply eliminate this part.

Hand Eunice the packet and ask her to deal the cards face down onto the table one at a time. "But deal them all over the place, Eunice. Put one here, another there, wherever. I know how hard it will be, but do your very best to be a little sloppy."

As directed, Eunice deals the cards at random face down onto the table. *Make sure you remember where the bottom card, the queen of spades, is.* Move the cards around a bit yourself, again keeping track of the queen of spades.

"Eunice, you and I are going to take turns eliminating cards. But first, I'm going to make a prediction as to what kind of card will be left."

Fan through the rest of the deck and pick out another black face card, but one not of the same value as the black face card on the table. In this instance, you have a black queen on the table, so you may choose as your prediction card either a black jack or a black king.

Place the card face down to one side, announcing that it's your prediction card, or, if you prefer, hand it to another spectator face down and ask her to guard it but not look at it.

"We'll let you make the first decision, Eunice. Please put your left hand on one card and your right hand on another. Then I'll choose one of those to eliminate." She covers the two cards. You choose one of them. Pick it up and set it aside, starting a pile. If she happens to cover the queen of spades, make sure you *don't* pick that one to eliminate. (It's important that Eunice be the first to cover two cards. This means that you'll be the last to pick from two cards, insuring the success of the trick.)

Now you put your right hand on one card and your left

hand on another. Make sure that neither is the queen of spades. "Eunice, choose one of these to eliminate."

She chooses one of the cards. You take it from her and set it on top of the first card eliminated.

Once more, Eunice covers two cards. You pick one—not the queen of spades, of course—and set it on the other eliminated cards.

Again, you cover two cards, making sure that neither is the queen of spades. Eunice picks one of them. You take it from her and add it to the pile of rejects.

Continue in this way until only two cards are left, one of which is the queen of spades. Eunice covers them. You pick the other card, of course, and add it to the pile.

"Now, let's take a look, Eunice, and see what card we chose. Please turn it over. Ah, the queen of spades. It's a black face card. Now let's see my prediction." Turn the prediction card over. "See? It also is a black face card." Pause to let this amazing revelation sink in. Announce dramatically and with great pride, "So I've correctly predicted that the choice would be... a black face card. Thank you so much."

Someone is bound to express curiosity as to the cards that have been eliminated. If so, say, "Really, that's not important." This is likely to inspire further inquiries. Eventually, give in, and show that all the eliminated cards are red spot cards of the same suit.

If no one wonders about the discard pile, pick it up and say, "So, we chose the only black face card from this whole packet of cards." If that doesn't stimulate a response, the entire group is in a state of catatonia.

Note: If you wish, this principle can be used in a straight prediction trick. In this instance, hand the deck to Eunice and ask her to remove all the cards of one suit and set the rest of the deck aside. Then have her shuffle the packet. As she does so, try to get a glimpse of the bottom card. Take the packet from her immediately.

But if you can't get a look as she shuffles, hold out your left hand to take the packet. Eunice places it in your hand. With your right hand palm down, lift the packet from your left hand. Tilt the packet forward slightly as you reach down to place it on the table. This should enable you to get a peek at the bottom card (Illus. 71).

Illus. 71

However you do it, make sure you know the value of the bottom card.

Set the packet onto the table, saying, "We'll get back to these cards in a minute. But first I have to find a prediction card."

Go through the deck and find a mate for the card you glimpsed on the bottom—that is, a card that matches it in value. If you glimpsed a seven on the bottom of the packet, you'd find a seven in the rest of the deck and place it face down on the table, making sure no one sees its face. Say, "This is my prediction card."

Proceed exactly as you do in the original version. Eunice deals the cards out all over the table. You keep track of the bottom card. And then you go through the selection process. The only difference is that there is no "sucker" climax at the end. You simply show that you have correctly predicted the chosen card.

Again, Eunice must be the first to cover two cards, and you must be the first to choose one. Otherwise, Eunice will make the last choice, which could be disastrous.

Yes and No

·····················

The principle behind this trick has been used fairly often. My version is intended to be both deceptive and amusing.

Roy is always good for a few laughs, so get him to help out. Ask him to shuffle the deck thoroughly. "Roy, I would like you to spell out a sentence, dealing into a pile one card for each letter. The sentence is: 'This is real magic.'"

Roy deals the cards as directed. You turn away.

"Please set the deck down, Roy, and pick up the pile you dealt off. Now, think of a small number—say, from 1 to 8. Quietly deal that many cards back onto the deck. Tell me when you're done."

When he's done, continue: "You chose a small number and dealt that number of cards back onto the deck. Now, please look at the card that lies at that number from the top of the pile you're holding. For example, if you thought of the number 3, you'd look at the third card from the top of your pile. Show the card around, but leave it at that number from the top of the pile. Be sure to remember your card, but you can forget that number you thought of."

Turn back to the group. "Roy, I'm going to try to determine what your card is through some key questions, all right?" Certainly it's all right. "When I ask you a question, Roy, you can tell the truth or you can lie. It's up to you. Each question should be answered yes or no. Ready?"

He is.

"First question: Do you always lie?"

Suppose he answers yes. Have him spell the word yes, transferring one card to the bottom for each letter in the spelling. If he answers no, he spells no, moving one card to the bottom for each letter. Obviously, he's transferring either three or two cards, but don't explain it that way.

You, however, keep track of the number on your fingers, with your hands casually hanging at your side. Here's how I do it: If his first answer is yes, I extend the thumb and two fingers on my left hand (Illus. 72). Let's suppose the next answer is also yes; I add three by extending all the fingers on

Illus. 72

my left hand and pushing out the thumb of my right hand (Illus. 73). And let's say that Roy answers no to the next question. I now have eight digits extended (Illus. 74).

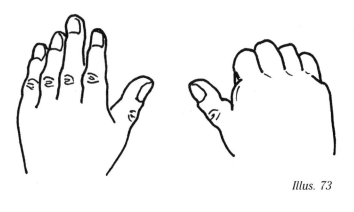

Illus. 73

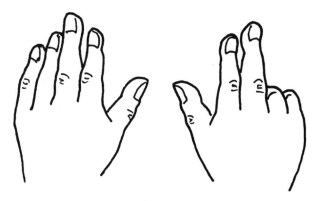

Illus. 74

When the number passes 10, I go back to the right hand. I mark the number 11, for instance, by extending my left thumb.

Eventually, you'll reach a count of 12, 13, or 14. His card will be at number 15, the number of letters in *This is real magic*.

If you stop at the count of 12, ask another question. If he answers no, have him spell "no," transferring cards as before. "From your answers, Roy, I believe that the next card is yours. This time, please tell the truth: What's the name of your card?" He names it. "Please turn over the next card." It's the chosen card, of course.

If he answers yes, he spells out "yes" as before. This time, you have him name his card and then turn the packet face up. Staring up at him is his chosen card.

If you stop at the count of 14, ask Roy the name of his card and have him turn over the next one.

When you stop at the count of 13, the handling is different. If you ask another question and Roy answers yes and transfers cards, his chosen card will become second from the bottom.

"I think we're close to your card, Roy. Hand me the top card of your packet, please." You take the card and study its back. "No, this isn't it." Set the card aside. "Could I have the bottom card." You study its back. "I don't think so." Set this one aside also.

"It must be the top card. Tell the truth this time, please: What's the name of your card?" He names it. You have him turn over the top card of the packet.

This Is Your Choice

In *Free Choice* I discussed the "magician's choice." A spectator apparently chooses an object, but actually it is forced on him. Here's one that I've worked out which seems very natural:

Illus. 75

You'll need a packet of three playing cards. Your best bet is to take three from an old deck. One of them should be a four, which has a lot of space in the middle. With a marker, print on the face of the four the words THIS IS YOUR CHOICE (Illus. 75).

To begin with, take the cards from your pocket, making sure no one can see the faces. Casually mix the cards face down and then deal them into a face-down row. You, of course, keep track of the four.

117

Say to Patricia, "Pick up two cards, please."

Let's assume that she leaves the "choice" card on the table. Take the other two from her. Point to the one on the table, saying, "Turn it over, please."

If one of the two she picks up is the "choice" card, say, "Hand me one, please."

If she retains the "choice" card and hands you the other, point to the card she holds, saying, "Turn it over, please."

If she hands you the "choice" card, say, "Excellent. Now, let's see what we have on your card." Show the other side.

You can add a bit of a "sucker" effect by quickly gathering up the other two cards face down, making sure you don't show the other sides. Naturally, the spectators will assume that all three have the message printed on them. You stall a bit, and then show that the other two cards have no printed message.

If you prefer, the same stunt can be performed with three calling cards.

Handkerchiefs

Most of these tricks demonstrate the passing of a solid through a solid. Various objects pass through a handkerchief: a glass, coins, another handkerchief. For some, this seeming repetition could be somewhat boring unless you have some excellent patter points. As you will see, each trick has a story to make the mysterious result even more interesting.

Cloth through Glass

Here we have one of the brilliant inventions of Gen Grant. You will not need an assistant—just two handkerchiefs, a medium-sized tumbler, and a rubber band. The glass should not taper at the bottom (Illus. 76).

Illus. 76

The glass is held in the right hand. The two handkerchiefs can be loosely stuffed into a pocket on your left side or laid over the right arm. The rubber band should be readily available—

either in a right-hand pocket or on a table to your right.

Gripping the glass near the bottom, hold it up so that all can see. "Here we have an ordinary glass," you declare.

Take one of the handkerchiefs in your left hand, saying, "And an ordinary handkerchief. And, of course, a really ordinary magician."

Lower the glass and stuff the handkerchief inside it (Illus. 77).

Illus. 77

Raise the glass to chest level.

You now cover the glass with the other handkerchief. First, take the second handkerchief with your left hand and briefly hold it in front of the glass, preparatory to moving it back and over the glass. In that second or so that the glass is concealed behind the handkerchief, let the glass pivot over so that it is now mouth down. Immediately, bring the handkerchief back toward you, covering the glass.

To pivot the glass properly, it should be held in your right hand as shown in Illus. 78. (For clarity, the handkerchief is not shown inside

Illus. 78

the glass.) Relax the grip slightly and the glass will pivot sideways, as shown.

Without stopping, bring the left hand back over the glass and grip it through the handkerchief. Lift the glass and the handkerchief with the left hand (Illus. 79). (Of course, the right hand has released its grip and is lowered.)

"Let's secure the glass so that the handkerchief can't possibly escape."

With the right hand, take the rubber band and place it over the upper portion of the handkerchief and glass. Illus. 80 shows the result.

"Is it possible that the handkerchief could escape?" Gesture at the glass with your right hand and say a few magic words.

Still holding the glass and handkerchief with the left

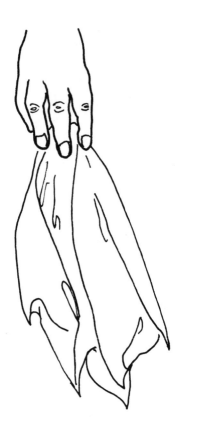

hand, reach under the handkerchief with your right hand. *Quickly*, pull the handkerchief from the glass, snapping it open as you produce it. Toss the handkerchief into the air and let it fall to the floor.

As soon as you toss the handkerchief, reach under the

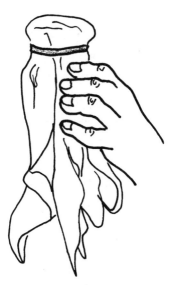

other handkerchief with your right hand and grip the glass near the bottom, ready once more to perform the pivoting move. With your left hand, pull on the handkerchief just enough to allow the rubber band to come loose.

Pivot the glass with your right hand, exactly as described above. Promptly pull the handkerchief (and rubber band) away with the left hand.

"What an escape!" you say, holding up the glass. "I'll tell you the secret. Actually, I cheated. I used a magical rubber band."

Pass out all the materials for examination.

The Supreme Kort

Milt Kort, magic's number-one authority, gave me permission to use this superb trick, which is based on a principle well known to magicians. It is similar to A Roll of Bills (page 79).

You will need a handkerchief, a large coin, and a somewhat smaller coin. Spread the handkerchief flat on the table so that it forms a diamond with one of the points aiming directly at you (Illus. 81). "I would like to perform for you a huge illusion," you begin to explain. "Unfortunately, the room is a little small, so we're going to have to make it a dinky little illusion. Nevertheless, we do have Houdini here." Display the large coin. "And here we have his beautiful assistant, Juanita." Display the small coin.

Place the large coin slightly above the center of the handkerchief (Illus. 82). "Houdini enters the trunk." Take the lower corner of the handkerchief and bring it upward, so that the top portion is about an inch beyond the portion beneath. In Illus. 83, dotted lines indicate the section of handkerchief that is beneath.

"The trunk is locked."

Place the small coin on the handkerchief so that it is on top of the large coin, separated of course by the fabric of the

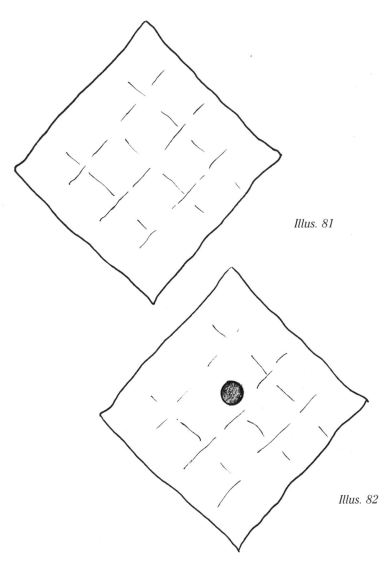

Illus. 81

Illus. 82

125

Illus. 83

Illus. 84

handkerchief. "Juanita sits on the trunk. And a beautiful cloth covers everything." Grasp the coins and turn them over as you fold the handkerchief upward about an inch (Illus. 84). Again, the coins are all turned over, and along with it the handkerchief as you fold it upward another inch or so. Continue this folding process until *one* tip flops over (Illus. 85). This is made easy because you left the lower portion an inch short when you folded the handkerchief over the large coin. (In the illustration, an arrow points to the tip; the other tip, of course, is beneath the handkerchief.)

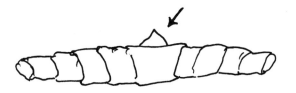

Illus. 85

Tap the handkerchief several times. "Only a few seconds passed, and when the beautiful cloth was removed..." Unroll the handkerchief. "...Houdini was sitting on top of the trunk..." The large coin is now on top (Illus. 86). Pick it up, display it, and set it aside. Lift back the top half of the handkerchief to reveal the small coin. "...and his lovely assistant,

Juanita, was *inside* the trunk."

Pause for a moment. "And next week, I'm going to saw a Barbie Doll in half."

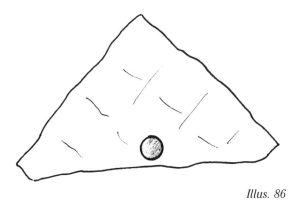

Coin through Handkerchief

There is nothing difficult about this trick, but the presentation must be casual and the timing perfect.

Hold a handkerchief and a large coin in your left hand. "We're about to try an experiment, ladies and gentlemen. But I find it extremely puzzling. I can never figure out whether I have a magic coin or a magic handkerchief. Maybe you can help me out."

Take the coin into the right hand and display it at your fingertips (Illus. 87). "Here's the coin."

Illus. 87

Cover the coin and your right hand with the handkerchief, so that the shape of the coin can be seen (Illus. 88). "And here's the handkerchief."

With the left hand, lift up the handkerchief at the top, as though you're taking the coin and handkerchief together (Illus. 89). Actually, the coin remains in the right hand. When the handkerchief is about halfway off the right hand, move your left hand and the handkerchief forward. The bottom half of the handkerchief comes off the right hand and conceals it.

Bring your left hand with the handkerchief back toward the right hand. Place the handkerchief on the coin, wrap-

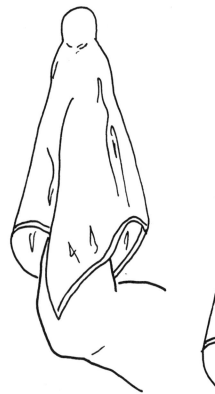

Illus. 88

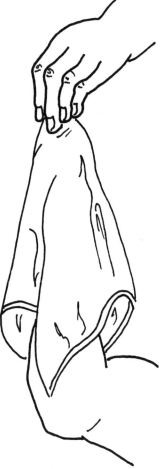

Illus. 89

ping the handkerchief around it, as shown in Illus. 90. (The coin is indicated by a dotted line.) Retaining this position, twist the handkerchief around several times, isolating the coin (Illus. 91). Make sure the coin does not pop out.

Pause as you explain, "So here we have the coin imprisoned by the handkerchief, or is the handkerchief sentenced to surround the coin?" Make whatever remarks you think appropriate while building to the climax.

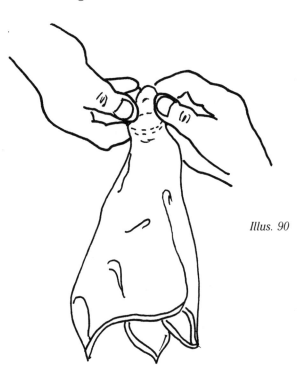

Illus. 90

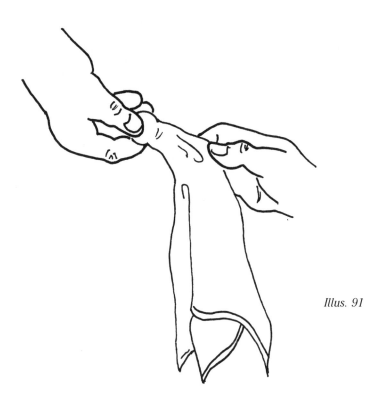

Illus. 91

Lower your hands and, with the right hand, push so that the coin gradually emerges from the handkerchief (Illus. 92). Apparently, it's coming right through the cloth. Finally, let it drop into the left hand.

Spread the handkerchief out and show that there's no hole in it. Then display the handkerchief in one hand and the coin in the other.

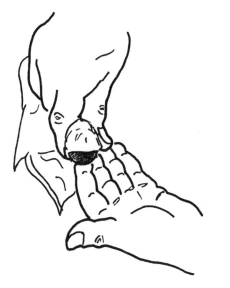

Illus. 92

"So which is magic—the coin or the handkerchief?"

Fall Out

For this fine trick, four medium-sized coins and a handkerchief are needed.

"For your entertainment, I'm now going to perform one of my less astonishing tricks." Hold up the handkerchief. "I'm going to convert this handkerchief into a bag."

133

Lay the handkerchief flat on a table. The handkerchief should form a diamond, with one of the corners pointing toward yourself. Note that in Illus. 93, I have identified the corners with letters and that corner C is the one pointed toward yourself. (To help you understand the folding procedure, the illustrations show the handkerchief as though it were a square of paper.)

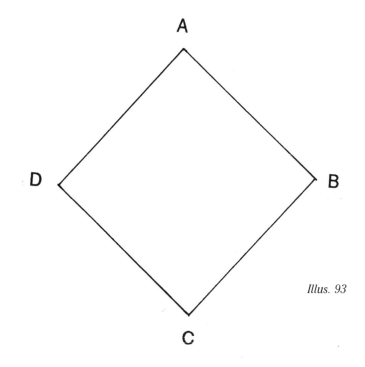

Illus. 93

Form the bag by bringing C up to A (Illus. 94).

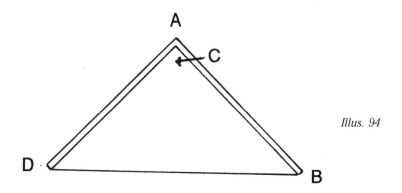

Bring D across to the opposite side so that it extends about two inches beyond the edge and about two inches lower than point A-C (Illus. 95).

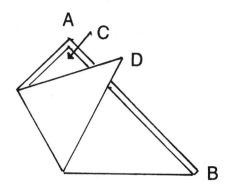

Illus. 95

In the same way, bring B across to its opposite side so that it extends about two inches beyond the edge and about two inches lower than point A-C (Illus. 96).

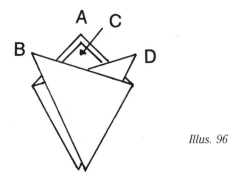

Illus. 96

With your right hand, grip point A-C between the second and third fingers. Then grasp points B and D between the right thumb and first finger.

Lift the handkerchief up, declaring, "And there you have it—a bag!" Pause. "And now for an even more impressive miracle, if you can imagine it."

With your left hand, show the coins. Drop them into the handkerchief between points A-C and B-D. Drop them close to point A-C. If you drop them too close to point B-D, they may fall right through the handkerchief.

Jiggle the handkerchief up and down, causing the coins to jingle. "As you can see, the handkerchief will also serve as a purse."

Bring your left hand beneath the handkerchief and coins. Jiggle the coins against the palm of the left hand. As you do this, twist your right hand counterclockwise, so that point A-C becomes *higher* than point B-D. The coins will drop into your hand.

If this doesn't seem to be working, move your right hand toward yourself and continue jiggling the coins. This should cause them to find their exit. After the coins fall into your hand, immediately pull the handkerchief up and away. Toss it into the air.

You now have a choice of conclusions. You can reach into the air with your left hand, letting the coins clink. Show them in your left hand and then drop them to the table. Or you can simply cup your hands, shake the coins so that they jingle, and then drop them on the table.

Either way, remark, "Maybe it wouldn't be such a good purse."

Do Not Fold

H old a handkerchief at its ends and twirl it till it becomes somewhat ropelike. Set it on the table.

"I'll bet that many of you are familiar with this bet: Can you take one end of the handkerchief in each hand and tie a knot in it without releasing the ends? It seems impossible, but it's really quite easy. Just tie a knot in your arms, and then transfer that knot to the handkerchief." This isn't quite accurate, but is fairly descriptive of what actually happens.

Fold your arms. Lean over to the left and take the *left* end of the handkerchief with your *right* fingertips. Tilt to the right and take the *right* end of the handkerchief with your *left* fingertips. Retaining your grip, unfold your arms; then bring your right hand to the right and your left hand to the left. You have just tied a knot in the handkerchief without releasing the ends. The trick is fairly well known and would not be worth mentioning except that it's a perfect introduction for an entirely different method.

If necessary, twirl the handkerchief again. Set it back on the table. "I wonder if anyone here could accomplish the same feat *without* crossing the arms. Let me show you a way."

Place your right hand palm up on the middle of the handkerchief (Illus. 97). With your left hand, take the right edge of the handkerchief and bring it over the right hand (Illus. 98). Push your right hand forward and then bring it back so that it passes over the portion held in the left hand. (The right hand is heading back toward you.)

Catch the left edge of the handkerchief with the right hand, either with the thumb and fingers or between the first two fingers of the right hand (Illus. 99).

Illus. 97

Illus. 98

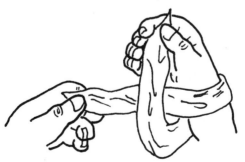

Illus. 99

Rubber Bands

O ver the past decade there has been an enormous increase of interest in tricks with rubber bands. The result is that there are many more such tricks, most of which are very good. Leading the way is the superb innovator and performer Dan Harlan, who has made a specialty of rubber band tricks.

The tricks in this section have stood the test of time and are extremely entertaining. Plus, you're provided another opportunity to perform spontaneously with materials that are readily available.

Just Passing Through

L et's start off this section with an amusing puzzler. This one probably works best with one large rubber band and one smaller one. The smaller one is shown shaded in the illustrations.

Take the two rubber bands from your pocket. Hold them together in your hand, briefly letting the group get a very quick glimpse.

"I'd like to show you something really peculiar about

these rubber bands. You see—" Look at the bands. "Oh, they're tangled up. Just a second."

Turn away briefly and perform the sleight as follows: Stick the larger rubber band inside the other (Illus. 100). With the right hand, grasp the larger rubber band at points A and B, and, with the left hand, grasp the smaller one at point C, as shown in Illus. 101. In both instances, the rubber band is grasped with the middle finger and thumb. It's important that the strands held in the right hand are slightly apart.

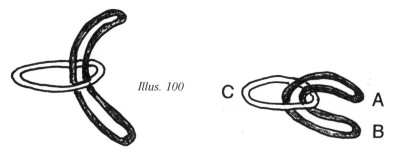

Illus. 100

Illus. 101

Turn back to the group, displaying the bands. "I opened up a new package of rubber bands and found these two stuck together. Did you ever have that happen?" Probably someone has. "Very odd."

Pull, slide, and stretch the bands every which way, just making sure that you *retain the original grip*.

141

"I don't know what to do. I guess my best bet is just to break one of them—like this!"

Pull the two hands apart as though trying to break a band. The fact that you've held the two strands apart in the right hand now makes it easy for you to release one strand. There is a snapping sound as the bands separate.

You appear satisfied. "There we are."

Then you notice that you're holding one complete band in each hand. Show the bands. Look perplexed while asking, "How do you suppose that happened?"

Breakout!

Not only is this a little-known trick, it is one of the best and easiest rubber-band tricks to perform.

You need two rubber bands. If they are of different colors, that's a plus. And for ease of performance, one should be fairly large. But neither is a requirement; two rubber bands of the same color and size will do just fine.

Display one rubber band in each hand (Illus. 102).

"I'd like to tell you about a man I once knew. His name was Stretch. Here he is."

Move the one in the left hand up and down. If there is a difference in the size of the two, this should be the larger one.

"Here's a story that he told me: 'One time, years ago, I robbed a bank. Through bad luck, I got caught and was tossed in jail. Because they knew how clever I was, they assigned me a special guard. They called him Rubberneck because he always had to see everything that was going on.'"

"We'll let this rubber band be Rubberneck." Move the one in the right hand up and down. "Now, let's put Stretch in jail where he belongs."

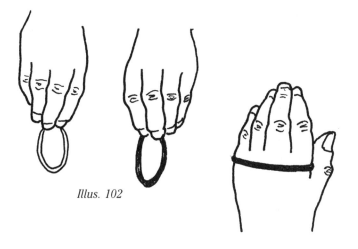

Illus. 102

Illus. 103

Place the Stretch band around the left hand at the base of the thumb, as shown in Illus. 103. (For clarity, this rubber band is shaded.)

"And let's make sure that Stretch is closely watched by the guard."

Put the other rubber band around the left hand also, about an inch to an inch and a half above the other (Illus. 104).

Your left hand should be positioned so that its back is uppermost. Close the hand into a fist. The back of the hand should have the Stretch band behind the knuckles and the Rubberneck band in front of the knuckles (Illus. 105).

While forming the fist, try to dig the left fingers under the Stretch rubber band, so that the view from the bottom would be as shown in Illus. 106. The movement should be undetectable. If you can't do this well, start by placing the Stretch rubber band a bit higher on the hand. If you still have trouble, drop your left hand to your side while making

Illus. 104

Illus. 105

some remark like, "It's virtually impossible for Stretch to escape."

To make sure no one can see the actual position, you should have the *right side* of your left hand to the audience; a look at the left side could give away the trick. To further conceal the trick, make sure you move your left thumb so that it is not beneath the fist, but alongside it, as shown in Illus. 107.

By this time, you should have your fingers properly placed. Bring your fist up and display it with the back uppermost. Make sure no one can see the underside.

Continue with your tale: "Stretch told me, 'Old Rubberneck was sure I couldn't possibly get away. But he forgot how brilliant I was. When I was in India, I learned how to walk right through walls. So I just concentrated… '"

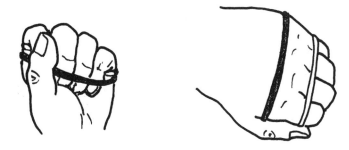

Illus. 106   *Illus. 107*

145

Lift up the Stretch rubber band with the right hand (Illus. 108).

"'. . . and *bam!*... '"

Move your left hand slightly forward. At the same time, slightly loosen the clenched fingers of the left hand and pull *back* on the Stretch rubber band. The slight movement of the left fingers is imperceptible; the illusion is that the Stretch rubber band passes right through your hand.

"'. . . I escaped.'"

Display the escapee in your right hand. Finally, the touch that makes the trick even more convincing. Please don't neglect this! Slowly turn your left hand over. Deliberately open your fingers, showing that Rubberneck is still there.

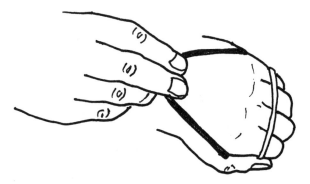

Illus. 108

"This demonstration worked, but I didn't quite believe the story. I think my friend earned his nickname because he really knew how to *stretch* the truth."

Note: In doing this trick, you could instead make up an excellent patter story using Houdini or some fictitious escape artist.

The Great Rubber Band Escape

For this escape trick, you'll need a rubber band, a dish towel (or some other object to conceal the operation), and string about three feet long.

"Presenting for your education, edification, and elucidation the famous rubber-band-and-string trick."

Display the rubber band and the string. Place the rubber band on the string and then ask someone to tie your wrists with the ends of the string.

"There you see it—the magic rubber band sitting on the magic string. Now, all we need is a magic dish towel and we can complete this mystical, magical miracle."

The rubber band and string are covered with the dish towel. (If available, a man's jacket or a sweater with buttons is probably better for cover.) After several seconds, you request that the dish towel be removed. The string is the same, but the rubber band has been removed and is held at your fingertips.

Shucks, there's nothing to it. Just slide the rubber band along the string. Then stretch it out so that it will pass over your fingers and end up resting on your wrist. Then work it down the wrist and under the string that binds your wrist. And there you are, holding it at your fingertips.

String, Cord, or Rope

Nearly all of the tricks in this section can be performed with string, cord, or rope. If using string or cord, you probably need a three- or four-foot length. If using rope, you need a length of at least five feet.

Many of these tricks also call for the use of a ring. Usually, a regular finger ring can be used, but I'd recommend using a metal ring three inches in diameter. It shows up much better and lends itself to easier handling. (These rings can be obtained at any craft store.)

I'd highly recommend that you combine some of the tricks using rings to make an entertaining routine. Pick out ones that you really like and either follow the suggested patter or develop a patter of your own.

For convenience, I'll assume that you're using string in nearly all of the following tricks. Actually, cord or rope could also be used in most instances.

Ring on a String 1: The Beginning

Let's start this section with something that's absolutely impossible: You magically place a ring on a section of string that is suspended between your tied wrists. This is a trick that always amazes me.

You'll need a piece of string at least three feet long and a ring of almost any size.

To start, borrow a ring from someone in the audience. (If you prefer—and I do—use your own ring, a

Illus. 109

metal one, three inches in diameter, which, as I mentioned, can be purchased at any craft store.) Have the ring examined by Grace, who is always very suspicious.

When Grace is finished, have her set the ring down. Hand her the string, saying, "Grace, I'd appreciate it if you'd tie my wrists with the ends of this string." She does so. If, as is quite likely, she ties a slip knot as she secures your wrists, make sure that she adds another knot; otherwise, all will be aware that the knot can be slid back.

"Please hand me the ring." Take the ring and explain, "By means of trickery, treachery, and deceit, I'm now going to sneak this ring onto this string... despite the fact that the string is securely tied to my wrists. It will be a miracle." Turn away from the group, muttering, "It *really* will."

Proceed with these steps:

(1) Push the center of the string through the ring. You now have a loop, as shown in Illus. 109. (For clarity, the looped portion is shaded in the illustrations.)

(2) Slip this loop *over* your right hand and beyond the portion of the string that binds your wrist (Illus. 110).

(3) From the side, grasp a strand of the loop that hangs below your wrist. Push this strand *under* the string that binds your wrist (Illus. 111).

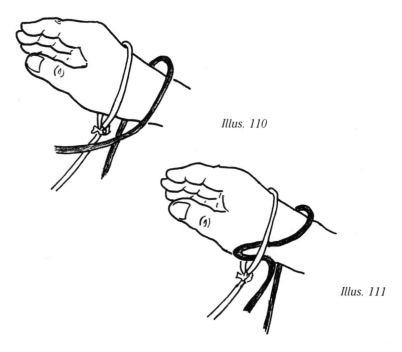

Illus. 110

Illus. 111

(4) Continue pulling this strand forward until you're holding a loop in your left hand. Bring this loop back over your right hand exactly as you did the first loop. (Study Illus. 112. This is *exactly* how the string should look prior to your bringing the loop back in the direction of the arrow. If the trick doesn't work, it will probably be because at this point you twisted the string.)

(5) Spread your hands apart. The ring is tied securely on the string (Illus. 113). Turn back to the group and show that this is so. But don't expect immediate applause. They may be thinking that perhaps the ring is not actually *on* the string.

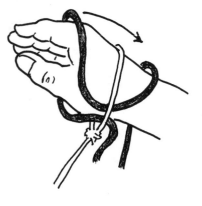

Illus. 112

Illus. 113

"Grace, please examine the ring and the string. See if you can get the ring off." Of course she can't. Nor can anyone else, as you extend the offer to other members of the group.

To get a smattering of applause, hold up your hands showing the ring dangling on the string, saying, "As I told you at the beginning—a miracle!"

Take your time at the end of the trick. The effect is definitely enhanced by the fact that, even after your hands are untied, the ring is still difficult to remove from the string.

Ring on a String 2: The Sequel

I n the next two tricks, a ring is removed from a string held at both ends by a spectator. In both instances the setup is identical:

(1) You'll need a three-foot length of string. Tie the end together, forming a closed loop.

(2) A ring of any size is placed in the middle of the doubled string.

(3) The string is looped over the spectator's thumbs, letting the ring dangle in the middle (Illus. 114).

This version is my own adaptation. It is quite simple and totally effective. To release the ring:

(1) With your left hand, grasp either string that is to your

right of the ring.

(2) With your right hand, remove the loop from the spectator's right thumb (to *your* left) and let go of it.

(3) *Instantly*, replace the loop by slipping the string in your left hand over that same right thumb.

(4) With your right hand, grasp either strand near the spectator's left thumb (to *your* right). Pull this strand sharply toward you. The ring will fall off the string, which remains on the thumbs.

Illus. 114

Ring on a String 3: The Return

I n the hands of my friend Wally Wilson, this trick is more than amazing; it's high-level entertainment.

As before, a spectator's thumbs hold a loop of string

from which a ring dangles. You place your raised left forefinger on the nearest string, well to the left of the ring (Illus. 115). With your right hand, grasp the nearest piece of string a few inches to the *left* of the ring. Bring this piece on *your side* of the left forefinger. Then take it forward (away from you) and place it clockwise around the spectator's left thumb (Illus. 116).

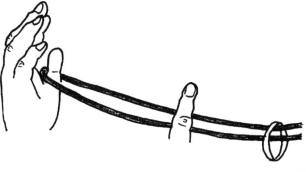

Illus. 115

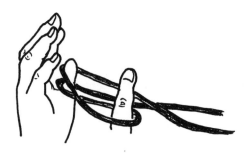

Illus. 116

Next, grasp with the right hand the back strand of string well to the *right* of the ring. Bring this strand to the left thumb and place it over the thumb clockwise (Illus. 117.) (Actually, counterclockwise also works, but the result is slightly different.)

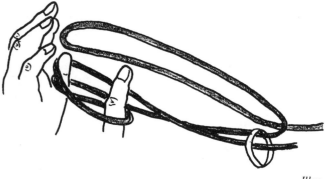

Illus. 117

Say to the spectator, "When I say, 'Now!' please pull your hands apart." Pause. Grip the ring with your right hand. Say, "Now!" and simultaneously let your left forefinger drop from the string.

Much to the spectator's astonishment, the string is still on his thumbs, and the ring is in your hand.

Incidentally, with all tricks of this type, be sure to let spectators examine the materials if they so desire. Otherwise, they might believe that the ring is not solid, or that the string is gimmicked in some way.

You might want to use this chestnut: "Do you want to know how I did that? Well, there's a hole in the ring." Pause. Then point to the open center of the ring. "See? Right there."

Ring on a String 4: The Legend Continues

I have never seen any reason to make this trick more fancy by using additional rings. The effect is strong when done rapidly and without frills. You'll need a ring, a three-foot string tied at the ends to form a loop, and a handkerchief or similar covering.

Start by threading the ring onto the doubled string (Illus. 118). Illus. 119 shows how to pull one end of the string (labeled X) through the other. Pull on end X so that the ring is secured (Illus. 120).

Illus. 118

Continue holding the end of the loop, letting the ring hang down. This enables everyone to see that the string is "tied" to the ring.

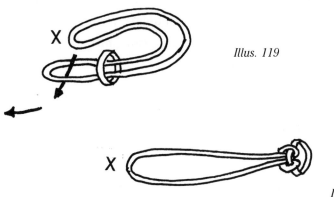

Illus. 119

Illus. 120

Ask a spectator to hold the portion of the string opposite the ring. (That's end X in Illus. 120.) He does so. You
cover the ring with your handkerchief and quickly remove it
from the string.

How? Illus. 121 shows the technique. In A, you loosen the
string from around the ring. In B, you pull the sides of the

C

Illus. 121

string outward. In C, you lift the loop off the ring. All that remains is to pull the string through the ring.

Finger Ring

To perform this trick, you must own a finger ring. Since the critical portion of the trick consists in holding the ring between your lips, it's not a good idea to borrow one. You also need a five-foot length of rope or strong cord.

Start by holding up the ring. "Using this ring, I will perform an astonishing feat which requires incredible dexterity, twisting, contortion, and lying."

Give the ring to Linda, asking her to hold it for a few minutes.

You'll need two more volunteers. Steve and George are both former Boy Scouts, so they're undoubtedly adept at tying knots. Ask them to help out.

Hand the rope to one of them, saying, "I'm going to put my hands behind my back. I'd like you two to tie my wrists so that I won't be able to get my hands loose."

As they do their job, you might make comments, like, "My hands don't have to be *that* secure," or, "Hey, hey, no trick knots!" or, "How about leaving a little circulation in my hands?"

They've finished their job; now it's Linda's turn. Say to her, "Select a finger, Linda—first, second, third, or fourth finger on either hand. If I'm confusing you, just point to one of your fingers." She does. "Let's see, that's the third finger on your left hand [whatever], so that's the one *I'll* use. In a moment, I'll go into the next room and try to put my ring on that particular finger. But first, Linda, I'd appreciate it if you'd put the ring between my lips."

She does so. You leave the room and, within seconds, return with your hands still tied and the ring on the designated finger.

Everyone is astonished. There may even be applause, especially if you pretend you're recovering from an agonizing effort. And, if you've performed well so far, Steve and George might even untie you.

Regardless, how did you do it? Years ago, I read a version of this trick in which the writer recommended that you push your tied hands to one side and twist your head in the same direction to the point of neck dislocation. Then the ring was dropped from the lips into one of the hands.

I don't think the writer really thought the problem through. It might be much easier to bend over a table and set the ring down. Then turn your back, pick up the ring, and put it on the appropriate finger.

If a table isn't available, you could use a chair.

Good Vibrations

You"ll need a length of string about three feet long. Tie the ends together, forming a closed loop.

Georgette loves to play cat's cradle, so she'll be happy to help with the string trick. "Georgette, please hold your right first finger up."

She does. Take the string and place one end of the loop over her finger (Illus. 122). Hold the other end of the loop with your left first finger, which is pointed down.

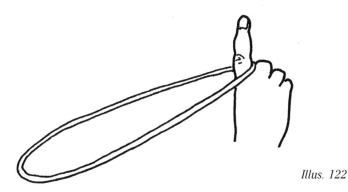

Illus. 122

Turn your right first finger down and reach to the left over the string. Bring your finger down until it is below the string at about the middle. Illus. 123 shows the setup.

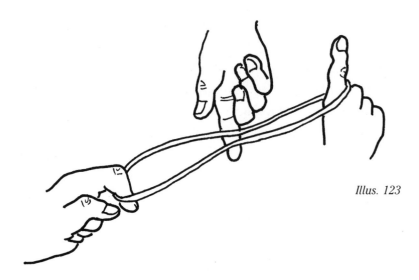

With your right first finger, pull both strands to the right, making it possible for you to place the loop held by your left first finger over Georgette's right first finger.

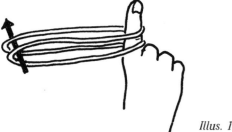

Illus. 124

The situation now is that there are two loops over Georgette's right first finger, while your right first finger now holds two strands of string. (See Illus. 124. The arrow indicates in which direction the right first finger is pointed.)

Bring your right thumb to the tip of your first finger, closing in the two strands.

Let's go back a bit. You placed the second loop over Georgette's finger and simultaneously closed in the two strands with your right thumb and first finger. *Instantly*, begin vibrating the string—that is, moving it violently and rapidly back and forth.

While doing this, explain, "A *real* magician told me you need the right vibrations to do this trick." Actually, you're moving the string so that no one can see the actual situation. Add: "Georgette, you'd better grab the tip of your first finger with your left hand."

She does this.

Continuing to vibrate the string, let loose one of the strands held in your right hand, and jerk the string away from Georgette's finger.

The string comes loose.

These Two Joined Together

H ow about *an absolutely impossible effect*? I thought you'd like the idea. All you need are two pieces of rope, each at least two feet long, and a dish towel or large handkerchief.

Display the two lengths of rope, saying, "These pieces of rope possess magical qualities, as I'll try to demonstrate."

Place the two lengths of rope on the table, side by side. Cover them with a dish towel so that the four ends can be clearly seen, but the rest of the ropes are concealed, as shown in Illus. 125. (For clarity, the ropes are labeled A and B, and A is shaded.)

"Keep your eyes on the ends of the rope, because—impossible as it sounds—I am going to try to link the two loops together."

Stand on the opposite side of the towel from where the ends are. Reach under the towel and do the following:

(1) Place middle portion of B over A (Illus. 126).

(2) Pull this portion to the right *under* A (Illus. 127). Let's assume that you move the bottom of Rope A slightly to the left, and the bottom of Rope B a bit to the right. Illus. 128 shows the interlocking illusion. (The arrows are at approximately the same position as in Illus. 127.)

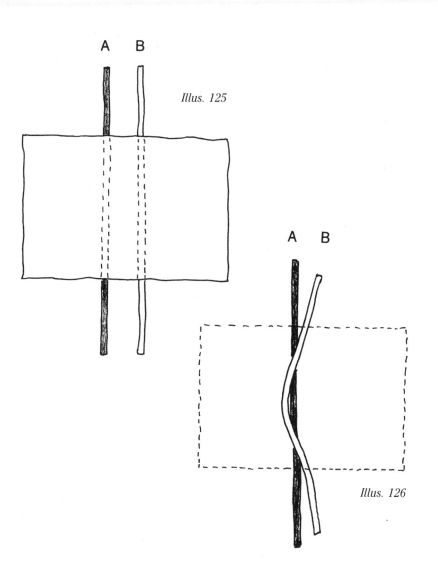

A   B

Illus. 125

A   B

Illus. 126

A   B

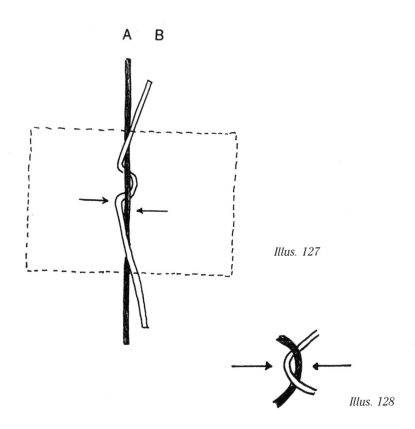

Illus. 127

Illus. 128

(3) Take one rope in each hand, retaining the linked appearance. Pull the ropes to your end of the towel. "Keep your eyes on the ends of the rope," you caution.

(4) Pull the loops beyond the towel and lift the towel and loops together, as shown in Illus. 129.

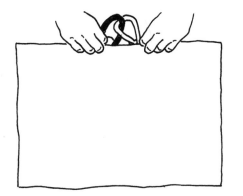

Illus. 129

"There they are!" Indeed, the ropes seem to be linked. Display them for only a second or two, however, before proceeding to the last phase.

(5) Let go of the towel and, as it drops, shake the ropes a bit, as though trying to keep the towel from clinging. Actually, you cause the ends of the rope to sort themselves out so that the ropes are *actually* linked.

The timing must be perfect on this last phase, so be sure to give it ample practice. Retain your grip on both ends as you move the right hand to the right. You form the knot automatically.

After practicing a bit, you'll be able to do this quite rapidly. Even after you've demonstrated this trick several times, spectators will find it almost impossible to duplicate.

Thimbles

Thimble tricks are snappy and astounding. Best of all, thimbles are convenient to carry. You need only three to do any of the tricks described. I highly recommend that you work out a routine that will last several minutes.

Where can you get colorful thimbles? Any magic shop and most craft stores carry a supply. I recommend that you carry two of one color and one of another color. If you can't find colored thimbles, buy plain ones and color them with spray paint.

Disappearing Thimble 1

Place a thimble on the first finger of your right hand and lay this finger on your left palm (Illus. 130). So that the audience can see clearly, you can either face left or face the audience with the fingers of the left hand extending toward the floor.

You will now appear to take the thimble into your left hand. Start by rotating both hands—the left hand clockwise, the right counterclockwise. While doing this, you close the right fingers, forming a *loose* fist around the right finger.

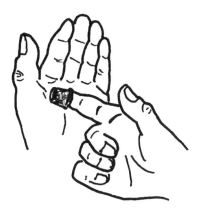

Illus. 130

Illus. 131

Illus. 131 shows the audience view.

Simultaneously, you bend the first finger down and grasp the thimble between your right thumb and third finger. Next, pull your left hand to the left, as though removing the thimble. You may tap the back of the left hand with your right first finger and then open the hand, showing that the thimble is gone.

The reappearance may be accomplished in any way you wish. Any of the coin reappearance ideas will work well. (See *Making a Coin Reappear*, *It's a Toss-Up*, *Good Catch*, *From Ear to Ear*, *"Oh, Here It Is"*, *In Your Ear*, *Slap 1*, and *Slap 2*, pages 32–37.)

Disappearing Thimble 2

O nce again, you start off with the thimble on the first finger of your right hand. This time, however, you stick your finger directly into a loose fist formed by your left hand. Again, Illus. 131 shows the position.

From this point, the trick follows the exact procedures as the preceding trick. Also, you make the thimble reappear as described above.

Thimple Thimble Thumb Palm

I f you can master the Thumb Palm, you can perform a wonderfully clever trick. Mastery of the thumb palm also opens the door to any number of other tricks with thimbles.

Place a thimble on the first finger of your right hand. Now quickly fold your first finger inward, placing the thimble at the base of your thumb. Instantly move your first finger back out. Illus. 132 shows where the thimble sits.

Practice this, not only with your right first finger, but also with your left first finger. You're now ready for the big time.

I'll first explain how many do the trick; then I'll tell you my way of making the move virtually undetectable.

Illus. 132

Beforehand, place a thimble in your right pants pocket and one in the left. The thimbles should be of the same color. To start, reach both hands into your pockets. In the left pocket, stick your first finger onto the thimble and then thumb-palm the thimble. In the right pocket, just stick your first finger onto the thimble.

Say, "Ah, here it is!" Apparently, you have been looking in both pockets for a single object.

Bring both hands out, but bring out the right hand just a bit before the left. And, as you do so, hold up the thimble, displaying it. The left hand falls to your side in a natural position with the fingers slightly curled.

"This is a magical jumping thimble. Let's see if it works."

Hold your hand so that the first fingers are pointing at the floor. On your right first finger is the thimble; on the left first finger is nothing (Illus. 133).

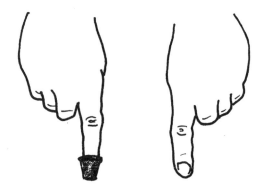

Illus. 133

There are now three ways you can perform the trick:

(1) Use this method if you're *really* fast. Hold your hands several inches apart. Move both hands rapidly side to side within a range of about three to four inches. As you do this, thumb-palm the thimble in the right hand, and produce the thimble on the first finger of the left hand. We'll call this *the basic move*. Bring both hands up so that the first fingers are pointing at the sky. "It *did* jump! Let's try it again."

Point the first fingers at the floor and repeat the trick. You can do this several times, but don't push your luck.

(2) Same positioning of hands. Same rapid side-to-side movements. *But*, after several of these movements, smack the first fingers together, and then quickly separate them. Just an instant before the fingers smack together, perform *the basic move*.

Complete the trick as described in the first version.

(3) This is by far the most deceptive method of the three. If you wish, you can combine this method with one of the others. If you do, I recommend that you save this method for last.

Assume the position for the first method, aiming the first fingers at the floor. Then, let your hands fall to your side, slightly cupped of course. As you do this, make some innocuous remark, like, "If this doesn't work, I'll give everyone here a coupon for a free thimble."

Near the end of your comment, bring your hands forward to assume the beginning position again. About halfway, perform *the basic move.* It's particularly deceptive in this instance because the hands are already slightly cupped.

Before the hands even reach the beginning position, begin moving them rapidly from side to side. At the same time, repeat, "Jump, jump, jump!"

Stop and show that the thimble has indeed jumped. The rapid movements prevent most people from noting that the thimble has already jumped. In fact, some will swear that they *saw* it move from one finger to the other.

Display the thimbles as in the other versions. Then assume the beginning position again. Pause, dropping your hands to your side, and say, "By the way, I forgot to ask if anyone wanted to see it again."

Perform it again. I don't recommend a third try.

Note: So you've performed the trick once with version two, and twice with version three, performing the trick three times in all. Now, how do you get rid of the extra thimble? Beforehand, you should have stuck a handkerchief in your right pocket. Now, reach in, leave the thimble there, and bring out the handkerchief. You can now mop your brow, blow your nose, or—my recommendation—perform the next trick.

Thimble through Handkerchief

"**D**on't you just hate it when you have a handkerchief with a hole in it?" Display the handkerchief, but not for too long. For now, you don't want the group to notice that there is no hole.

Hold the handkerchief in your left hand, and, as usual, display the thimble on the first finger of the right hand.

Bring the handkerchief in front of your right hand, preparatory to placing it over the thimble and hand. As soon as the handkerchief affords cover, thumb-palm the thimble, raising your first finger back up. Place the handkerchief over the first finger, which is presumed to still have the thimble on it. As you do this, insert your *second* finger into the thimble.

You brought only five or six inches of the handkerchief over your first finger, because you need to tuck a portion behind the first finger so that all the fingers except the first finger are outside the handkerchief (Illus. 134). You do this under the guise of arranging the handkerchief so that everything is adequately covered.

Give a quick side-to-side move of your entire right hand. Simultaneously, abruptly raise your left second finger so that it's right behind the first finger—or as close as you can

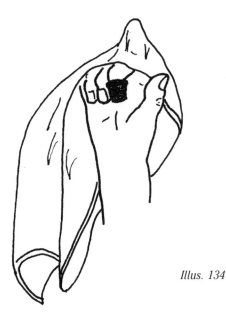

get. (Check this action in a mirror; only the thimble should show, not any of the second finger. To make sure, when you arrange the handkerchief, pull it up a bit from the first finger.)

"Look at that!" you declare. It looks as though the thimble has penetrated the handkerchief. But you don't want to waste a second, because you don't want anyone to see the true situation. *Promptly*, with the left hand, move the thimble so that it rests on top of the right first finger (through the handkerchief, of course).

Continue holding the thimble and handkerchief with

your left hand, as you attempt to get your second, third, and fourth fingers under the handkerchief. Do this by folding your fingers in as far as possible *and*, at the same time, moving your hand slowly back and forth, helping the handkerchief fall behind the hand. At the same time, say, "There it is—right through the hole in the handkerchief."

Now, you can turn your right hand to show all sides of the handkerchief.

"It's magic time! I'm going to repair that hole in the handkerchief."

Wave your left hand over the handkerchief, muttering your favorite magic words. Remove the thimble and display the handkerchief. Finally, pass it out for examination.

Jumping Thimbles

The easy sleight featured in this trick is often used with a plastic bandage or a rubber band. This time you'll use three thimbles. Let's suppose that two are red and one is blue. Unobtrusively place them on the fingertips of your right hand. Place a red one on the first finger, a blue one on the second finger, and a red one on the third finger. Hold out the first and second fingers, while the others are folded in.

Turn to your left and hold out your left arm. Place the

first two fingers of your right hand on your left forearm, as shown in Illus. 135.

You now have a choice of two moves, whichever seems to work best for you:

(1) Move the right hand up and down several times. Finally, fold in the first finger and extend the third finger and bring these two fingers to rest on the left arm (Illus. 136). Evidently, the two thimbles have exchanged places. But don't let the group observe them for too long.

Repeat the up-and-down movements, folding in the third finger and extending the second finger. Return the two to your arm, showing that the thimbles have jumped back again.

I wouldn't recommend repeating the trick. Simply put your right hand into your pocket and leave all three thimbles there. Bring your hand out again. If you wish to show another thimble trick, say, "Oh, I almost forgot; I have another trick you might like." Reach into your pocket and take out one of the thimbles.

(2) The second method differs only in the direction of the motion. Instead of moving the right hand up and down, you move it back and forth—that is, you move it rapidly toward the left for several inches and then move it back.

Check both moves out in a mirror and see which one you prefer.

Note: Some performers prefer to make only *one* move.

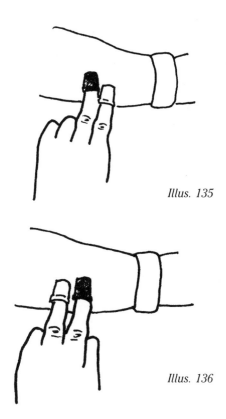

Illus. 135

Illus. 136

They move the right hand swiftly, going either up and down or sideways. As they start the swift return to the arm, they perform the switch with the fingers.

Try this way, too. You may like it.

Tableware

The magician should be ready at all times to amaze and amuse. Whether eating at home or out, you can amaze with any of these entertaining tricks involving things you can readily find at the dinner table.

A Little Juggle

Hold your right first finger up, the back of your hand toward onlookers. Take an olive and place it on top of your first finger. Much to the astonishment of onlookers, you balance it there.

Nothing to it! Secretly place a toothpick along the length of your left first finger, holding it in place with your right thumb.

The back of your hand is toward the group as you stick an olive onto the toothpick, apparently balancing the olive on your first finger (Illus. 137). As you place the olive on the finger, push the toothpick up slightly, making it easy to pierce the olive. Obviously, you only push the olive until the toothpick pierces it slightly; you don't want to destroy the balancing illusion.

After several seconds of balancing the olive, lower your hand. Draw the toothpick down with your left thumb as you remove the olive and pop it into your mouth. Previously, you made sure your handkerchief was in your left pocket. You now reach in and take it out with your left hand. While doing so, leave the toothpick in the pocket.

Naturally, you wipe your hands off with the handkerchief.

Illus. 137

Rolling Spoon

I f you don't try another trick in this book, try this one. It's absolutely eerie!

Years ago, a certain kind of skeleton key could be used to accomplish a similar effect, but I don't believe that this effect is nearly as strong as that obtained with a tablespoon.

To see how this trick works, place a tablespoon on your extended fingers, with the humped side of the spoon *up*, as shown in Illus. 138. Note that this side is *off* the hand. The

Illus. 138

tablespoon may want to turn over immediately. This means that you must tip the hand down slightly. With a bit of trial and error, you'll discover exactly the point at which the spoon will lie there stable.

Wave your other hand over the spoon. As you do so, gradually and imperceptibly tip your hand up. With a minimum of movement—practically none, in fact—the spoon will roll over toward you (Illus. 139). The first few times, and maybe all the time, it will look magical *to you*. Imagine the effect on an audience.

How do you use this marvelous trick? You can tell this kind of story: "A certain tribe of Indians [your choice] used to use eating implements to tell the future. I've found that we can accomplish the same thing with a certain kind of

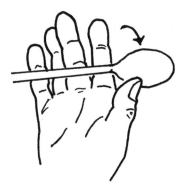

tablespoon, providing we make the proper mystical waves over it." Or, " ... providing we say the magical Indian words."

Place the spoon on your hand. Say to Ellen, "Please ask the spoon a question. If the answer is no, the spoon will stay as it is. If the answer is yes, the spoon may move slightly."

Note how you underplay the movement of the spoon. When it eventually answers yes, you'll hear oohs and ahs from the audience.

Ellen asks a question. Depending on your mood, you have the spoon answer yes or no. Do this a few more times, making sure there are at least a few yes answers.

Quit while the audience is still amazed.

Notes:

(1) If someone says that the spoon made an incorrect

answer, say, "I said that the spoon would answer your questions; I *didn't* say that the spoon was particularly intelligent."

(2) You'll probably find this out for yourself soon enough, but *don't try to make the spoon roll back*. After it has rolled over, pick it up, turn it over, and replace it on your hand with the humped side up.

(3) It is best to try to prevent others from experimenting with the trick. Obviously, you can't prevent this if other tablespoons are lying about. But you can at least put *your* spoon away. It will help also if you distract the group by immediately moving to another stunt.

A Hard Roll

This is not exactly a trick, but it sure is fun.

Suppose you're sitting at the dinner table or at a table in a restaurant. Move your chair in close to the table. It should be easy to surreptitiously put your right arm several inches under the table.

Pick up a roll with your left hand. Look it over and comment, "I wonder if these are fresh."

Tap the roll on the table a few times and, in perfect synchronization, tap the knuckles of your right hand on the underside of the table.

Bouncy Food

T his one will take some practice.

You're seated at a table, preferably at the head. Pick up a biscuit, a roll, an apple, an orange, whatever.

Get the group's attention by saying something like, "Have you ever noticed how high one of these things can bounce?" Then throw the object to the floor. It will bounce off the floor with a little bang and fly high into the air. When it comes down, you catch it. Replace it on the table and continue with the meal.

You don't *actually* throw it to the floor, of course. But, with the object in your right hand, you make a throwing motion toward the floor, letting your hand go out of sight, well below the level of the top of the table. The object remains in your right hand. Pausing only a fraction of a second, you slap your right foot against the floor, simulating the sound of the object hitting the floor.

Immediately, you *flip* the object into the air. In doing this, you don't move your arm. You simply "break" your wrist.

Illus. 140 shows the action below the level of the table.

When the object comes down, catch it. Continue your meal as though nothing had happened. Don't repeat the stunt; the group will probably catch on.

Please don't try this without giving it considerable practice. It's too good a stunt to goof up.

Illus. 140

Pencils

You find pencils everywhere, so why aren't there very many pencil tricks? This is a mystery, especially since many of the pencil tricks are entertaining and extremely mystifying. Here are five of the very best.

Pencil Hop

If you're going to perform a number of pencil tricks, this snappy Stewart James stunt is an excellent way to start off.

Stand with your right side toward the group. Hold your right hand out palm down. With your left hand, place a pencil, point up, between your right *second and third* fingers (Illus. 141). The other fingers are folded in.

The group will assume that the pencil is being held in a normal position, between the first and second fingers.

"Notice, please, that the point of the pencil is *up*, whereas the eraser end is *down*. Watch!"

You make a quick up-and-down motion and, at the same time, snap your right first finger forward. The ends of the pencil reverse. You're now holding it between the first and second fingers with the others fingers folded in (Illus. 142). Let the audience get a good look at this.

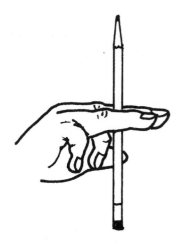

Illus. 141

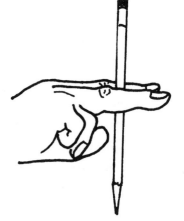

Illus. 142

188

"As you can see, the pencil has been magically reversed. Now the eraser is on top, and the point on the bottom."

To perform the trick, the top of the pencil should be tilted a bit to the right, enabling your first finger to come in on the *right* side and rapidly revolve the pencil. You can either tilt the pencil when placing it in the right hand, or, just before snapping the right finger out, tilt the pencil by moving the *second finger* upward.

This is another trick that you'll want to practice in front of a mirror.

Penetrating Pencil

C an you believe that a trick invented in 1927 could be as clever and as contemporary as anything conceived today? I think this is absolutely true of yet another fooler by Stewart James.

All you need are a pencil and a handkerchief. Also, make sure no one is standing behind you.

Start by cupping your left hand and holding it at about shoulder level (Illus. 143). Then place a handkerchief over it with most of the handkerchief on the side of the spectators; in fact, on your side, there should be only four or five inches.

Illus. 143

As you place the handkerchief on your left hand, say, "And here we have a magic handkerchief. I can put as many holes in it as I want, and it *instantly* repairs itself."

Take the pencil in your right hand so that the eraser end is down. "Let's form a little pocket."

You don't want the audience to see precisely what you're doing, so tilt your left hand back toward you a bit. Then push the eraser end of the pencil down into the middle of the handkerchief, forming a pocket in your cupped left hand. As you do this, the hem on your side of the handkerchief rises. Simultaneously raise your left thumb. As soon as you can see the tip of your left thumb, stop pushing down with the pencil.

Pull the pencil out and reverse it so that the point end is down. Apparently you now push the pencil right through the handkerchief. Actually, you push it down between your left thumb and the handkerchief. (As soon as it's possible, lower your left thumb.) When the pencil emerges below the handkerchief, press on it with the left thumb to hold it in place. Immediately, release the grip with your right hand and bring the right hand down to grasp the emerging pencil.

Pull the pencil through and place it *sideways* in your mouth. Pull the handkerchief off your hand and show that there is no mark. In fact, you may pass it out for inspection. Chances are, no one will be interested in inspecting the pencil.

The Semi-Disappearing Pencil

So far, you've been just a bit too serious with your presentations. It's time you provided a little chuckle— maybe even a guffaw. Fortunately, Martin Gardner has provided us with the perfect stunt for this situation.

You'll need a pencil, a handkerchief, and some practice. Hold the pencil in your right hand with your first two fingers and thumb, gripping it near the point. Illus. 144 shows the position from your point of view. You should be holding the pencil several inches in front of your face, at about chin level. (A few attempts will show you the proper position.)

With your left hand, grasp the handkerchief, bringing it

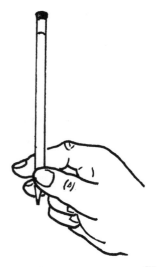

Illus. 144

Illus. 145

above and back to the pencil, as though to cover it (Illus. 145). As soon as the handkerchief conceals your right hand and the pencil, tilt the pencil back toward you. The easiest way to do this is to release the grip of the *second finger*; this almost automatically tilts the pencil back.

If you have positioned everything properly, the eraser end of the pencil should be near your mouth. Take the end between your teeth and, instantly, raise your right first finger to substitute for the pencil.

It goes without saying that the end of your finger doesn't closely resemble the end of the pencil, but it will substitute nicely for a few seconds.

Illus. 146

Ready for the thrilling climax? With your left hand, whip the handkerchief to one side. In the same instant, open your hand wide, palm toward the group. Your hand should be directly in front of your face, concealing the lower portion, including your mouth. The pencil, of course, is completely hidden (Illus. 146).

Shake the handkerchief so that it becomes perfectly clear that the pencil is not there. Then very slowly lower your hand, revealing the pencil sticking out of your mouth.

If this doesn't get at least a chuckle, the entire group must have just come from a funeral.

The Magic Pencil

For a change of pace, perhaps you should try another amusing trick. Basically, you'll be doing this for one person; if others are present, however, they will certainly enjoy it, and some might even be fooled.

Nothing embarrasses Wally, so he'd be the ideal assistant.

"Wally, please hold your hand out palm up." Place two coins of different values on his outstretched hand. "I'm going to make one of these coins disappear. You get to choose which one."

He signifies one of the coins.

Hold up a pencil that you should be gripping near its point. "This is a magic pencil. Three taps with this pencil, and the coin will be gone."

Touch the coins with the pencil, saying, "Watch carefully now."

Raise the pencil a foot or so; then bring it down and, with the eraser end, tap Wally's palm, saying, "One." Raise the pencil near your head on the right side and then bring it down, again tapping Wally's palm and saying, "Two." Raise the pencil once more and, this time, place the pencil behind your right ear. Bring your hand down to his palm in an effort to tap his palm. Say, "Three," but stop and look at your hand in bewilderment. "Hey, where's the pencil?"

As you bring your hand down the third time, be sure to turn your head somewhat to the right so that Wally can't see the pencil.

Show that both hands are empty. Point to the floor. "Is it on the floor?"

If Wally looks down, take the pencil from behind your ear and stare at it in puzzlement.

If Wally doesn't look away, you may have to turn your head so that he can see the pencil behind your ear. He may notice right away, or he may not. If he doesn't, you might say, "I can't imagine what happened to it, can you?" He's bound to see it eventually.

When he does, take the coins from his hand and put the pencil away, saying, "Nothing seems to be working the way it should. Let's try something else."

Now you can perform a *real* trick.

Perfect Misdirection

I n some respects, this is the same trick as the preceding one, but with a totally different approach. This is a favorite of Michael Ammar, a master of magic of all sorts.

Again, we'll use a pencil, although you *could* use a straw, a big pretzel stick—anything that can substitute for a wand.

Hold the pencil up in your right hand, saying, "This seems to be an ordinary pencil, right? But actually it has magical powers. I'll show you."

With your left hand, pick up any small object that can be concealed in the hand. Let's assume that you pick up a straw. Turn your hand palm down so that you're holding the straw as

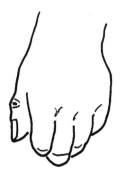

Illus. 147

shown in Illus. 147.

"Let's count it out and see what happens."

Now you perform the same counting routine as described in the previous trick. The only difference is that this time you slip the pencil into the back of your collar (Illus. 148).

"Say, what happened to the pencil?"

Someone will probably notice. It doesn't matter. Make a half turn to the left, letting your left hand drop naturally. With your right hand, point to the pencil stuck behind your collar.

At the exact instant that everyone's attention is focused on the pencil, drop the straw into your pocket—the jacket

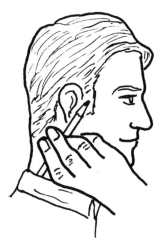

Illus. 148

197

pocket, or, if you're not wearing a jacket, the pants pocket.

As you take the pencil from your collar, bring the left hand up. Place it into its previous position. The misdirection is so strong that everyone will assume that it's been like this the entire time.

"That was just a dumb trick. Let's try some real magic."

With the pencil, tap the back of your left hand once. Turn the left hand over, showing that the straw has disappeared.

Other Objects

Many persons expect a magician to be able to perform a trick with nearly any object. It's really a shame to have to disappoint them. And if you can't fulfill a request, it doesn't do your reputation much good.

Fortunately, you'll seldom get such a request. But you often will perform spontaneously with an object that is lying about. Hardly anything seems more magical. "He just picked up the key and made it disappear!" This extemporaneous magic creates the impression that you can do practically *anything*.

The first three tricks in this section can be performed on virtually any occasion and are real reputation-builders. The others require some preparation, but are well worth the modest effort required.

Easy Vanish 1

This trick and Easy Vanish 2, which follows, are methods of causing small objects to disappear: a pocket knife, a key, etc. Anything of any shape will do, providing that it is longer than it is wide, and that it is no more than 3 inches long and about an inch and a half wide. (On occasion, you might make objects somewhat larger than this either in length or width disappear, but when doing so, you're definitely taking your chances.)

Despite the simplicity of these disappearances, they are not well known, even among magicians.

Let's assume that you're going to make a key disappear. In the first trick, you are going to pretend to place the key in the left hand, but actually retain it in the right hand. The question is this: Why did you decide to put the object in the other hand? The answer is: Because your handkerchief is in your right-hand pocket, and you need it to cover your left hand before performing the magic. Of course, neither question nor answer is actually voiced, but it is helpful to have logical (or semilogical) reasons for the magical things you do. (See the discussion in the introduction to *Coins*, page 12.)

Display the key in your right hand, gripping it between the outer joint of the middle finger and the palm near the base of the thumb (Illus. 149). Your left hand should be held palm up, the fingers very slightly cupped. At this point, both hands are held palm up, and both are slightly cupped.

Place the right hand beneath the left, letting the left fingertips rest on the left side of the right palm (Illus. 150). With the edge of the right palm, close up the left hand, evidently dropping the key in the process. Actually, of course, the right hand retains the key *in exactly the same grip.*

Move the left hand forward as the right hand drops. You may make the key reappear any way you wish. In this scenario, you put your right hand into the right pants pocket, drop the key there, and remove a handkerchief. As you shake out the handkerchief, make sure that all can see the palm of your hand. But don't make it too obvious.

Place the handkerchief over your left hand. Say a magic word or two. Remove the handkerchief, and show that that hand is empty.

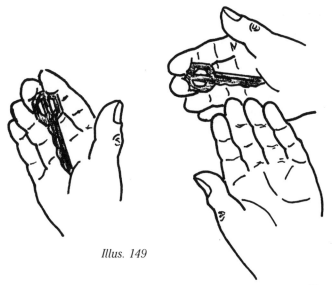

Illus. 149

Illus. 150

Easy Vanish 2

This is so similar to the above that it might be termed a variation. Both are effective; it's just a question of which one you prefer.

In this version, start with both hands palm up and the key sitting on the tips of the left fingers (Illus. 151). As you will see, it's important that the key extend a bit beyond the fingers on both sides.

The right hand is now going to come over and close the left hand. I have no idea why the right hand should be needed for this service, but the action seems to play well.

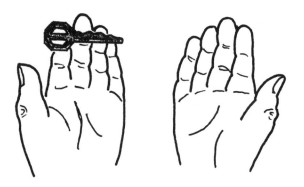

Illus. 151

The right hand approaches the left hand from below and moves upward, grasping the key between the third finger and the palm (Illus. 152). This is pretty much the same grip as described at the beginning of *Easy Vanish 1*. The right hand then proceeds to close the left hand in *exactly* the same way as described above. And the right hand drops as the left hand moves forward.

The trick is completed by causing the key to reappear somewhere, or by performing the trick with the handkerchief.

Note: With either of the two vanishes just discussed, you may tap the back of your left hand with the first finger of the right hand. Or you may point at the left hand with your right first finger. Just watch the angles.

Illus. 152

Spheres of Action

This Stewart Judah invention is among the best impromptu tricks.

In magic, an object that is secretly placed somewhere for a later appearance is called a "load." The load in this case is a small round object like a plum, a table-tennis ball, or an olive. The object should not be too large; some practice will indicate what size object can be used. Let's assume that you're using a table-tennis ball. Ahead of time, place this into your right pants pocket. Also in the pocket you should have a small ball wadded up from a quarter of a page of newspaper. Place the ball in your right pants pocket on top of the load.

To begin, show a page of newspaper. Tear it into quarters. Take three of the quarters and wad them up into small balls. Look for a place to put them so that you can set aside the newspaper. Not seeing one, place them in your right pocket, where you already have a wadded ball. Don't explain anything; just do it. Set aside the newspaper.

Reach into your right pocket and finger-palm one ball. (Here you use the Finger Palm described in *A Wad of Money*, page 75. This consists of holding the wad by the third and fourth fingers. See also *The Finger Palm*, page 16.) Bring out the other three balls and toss them onto the table.

"Three ordinary paper balls," you explain. "The problem is this: They all came from the same sheet of newspaper. You'll see what I mean."

The trick has four phases, including a wonderful surprise ending:

(1) With both hands, place the balls in a line on the table (Illus. 153).

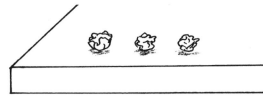

Illus. 153

With your right hand, pick up one ball between your first two fingers and the thumb. Toss this ball into the left hand, closing the hand as it accepts the ball.

The motion used in tossing the ball is quite important. The right hand approaches from the front (Illus. 154). It moves back and drops its ball, moving quite close to the left hand. The left hand starts closing as the right hand passes over it. This shields the dropping of the ball (or balls).

You have tossed one ball into the left hand. Pick up another, and, with the same motion as used before, toss both that ball and the palmed ball into the left hand. Close the left hand.

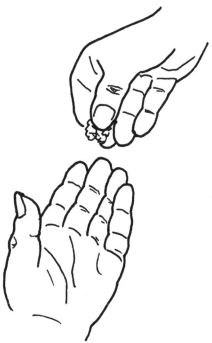

With your right hand, pick up the remaining ball and place it in your right pants pocket, saying, "We'll take this ball away from his friends." Immediately finger-palm the ball and bring your hand out.

With the right first finger, point to the left hand, saying, "It always returns." Open the left hand, showing the three balls.

(2) As before, toss the three balls onto the table and line them up. Pick up one ball in the right hand. This time, toss *both* balls into the left hand. Pick up a second ball, casually turning your hand palm-outward so that all can see that there is no second ball there. Toss the ball into the left hand.

Pick up the third ball and place it into your pocket, repeating, "We'll take this ball away from his friends." Finger-palm it and bring it from your pocket. Point with your right hand to the left, saying, "But all three are from the same sheet of newspaper." Open the left hand, showing the three balls.

(3) Drop the three balls onto the table so that all can see them. With one sweep of the left hand (or as close as you can come to it), pick up all three balls. "As you probably know, this little stunt is as old as... yesterday's newspaper." As you speak, get one of the balls in the finger-palm position in your left hand. Actually, this should happen almost automatically from the manner in which you sweep up the balls.

Toss two of the balls into your right hand, retaining the finger-palmed ball in your left hand. This motion is the same as that used when tossing a ball from your right hand to your left. The situation: One ball is finger-palmed in your left hand. The two balls have joined the one that was originally finger-palmed in your right hand, so there are now three balls held in your closed right hand.

Open your right hand to show three balls there.

Drop the three balls onto the table.

Hold your left hand in a loose fist. Pick up one ball with your right hand and push it into the side of the fist (Illus. 155). Say, "One."

Illus. 155

Push another into the fist in the same way, saying, "Two."

With your right hand, pick up the third ball, and display it at your fingertips. Place it in your right pocket. Leave it there.

After you remove your right hand, turn it outward in a gesture while remarking, "That ball just likes to travel." This subtly shows that your right hand is empty.

Open your left hand, showing the three balls.

(4) Roll the balls out onto the table. "Let's try it again. I put one ball in my pocket." Pick up a ball with your right hand, display it at your fingertips, and place it in your pocket. At this point, take the table-tennis ball (or whatever your "load" happens to be) and finger-palm it.

Remove the right hand from your pocket, pick up a ball, and display it at your fingertips. The load, indicated by the arrow in Illus. 156, will not show.

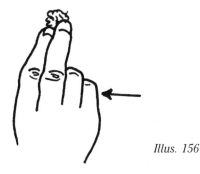

Illus. 156

Apparently place the ball into your left hand. Actually, drop the load into the left hand. The motion you use is the same as before, but, as the load is dropped, the left hand is tilted back somewhat to better conceal the load. Close the left hand as much as possible.

With the left first finger, point to the ball on the table, saying, "We have one ball left on the table." At the same time, drop your right hand to your side and finger-palm the ball it holds.

The situation: Two balls are in your pocket, one ball is on the table, one ball is finger-palmed in your right hand, and the load is in your left hand.

Now your left hand drops casually to your side; simultaneously the right hand picks up the ball remaining on the table. Display it at your fingertips and place it in your pocket. Leave both balls there and remove your right hand from the pocket.

With a casual gesture, show that your right hand is empty. Now you're going to bring your left hand forward. Point to it, saying, "How many balls do you suppose I have here?"

As far as the spectators are concerned, you have two balls in your pocket and one in your left hand. They suppose, however, that you have performed some sort of skulduggery and that it's possible that more than one ball is in your left hand. So you're quite likely to get a variety of answers.

If someone is kind enough to say, "One," you open your hand, showing the load. "That's right... just one!"

If no one says, "One," you open your hand, saying, "No... there's just one!"

Take My Card... Please

The aspiring magician is always looking for a good way to get his calling card into the hands of a potential customer. Even if you're not looking for business, this is a superb trick. It's a favorite of Michael Ammar, a marvelous performer and, beyond a doubt, the best magic teacher around.

You should use about 20 business cards. Hold them in your hand with the printed sides up. Take off about 10 cards and turn them face down on top. Now, no matter which way you remove the cards from your pocket or wallet, you will be looking at blank cards. (Incidentally, if you can see printing through the cards, do not use them.)

Let's say that you want to give someone your business card. Take out your packet, commenting, "My business cards are really strange; they don't have any printing on them." Fan through six or seven cards so that all can see that they're blank. Close up the packet and turn it over. Fan through six or seven cards on the other side, saying, "See what I mean?"

Fan down about three cards and, with your right hand, remove the fourth card. Your left hand holds the remainder of the cards. Place these in your pocket. Place the card you removed onto the fingers of your left hand (Illus. 157).

Turn your left hand over and, as you do so, your fingers naturally turn the card over so that the blank side is still up. Practice this move a bit so that you don't give the audience a glimpse of the printed side of the card.

Push your thumb against the side of the card, pushing it out the left side of your hand (Illus. 158). Apparently both sides are blank.

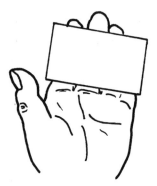

Illus. 157

Again, take the card and place it on the left hand, only this time place it on the palm. Now, when you turn your hand over, the card does not turn over, and the printed side is up.

Ammar recommends that you now act as though you're typing on the back of the left hand with your right fingers, explaining, "We can't get any

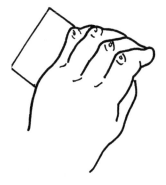

Illus. 158

print on the card unless we type."

As before, push the card out the left side of your hand with your left thumb. This time, the printing side of the card shows up. You have magically put your name, address, and phone number onto the blank card. Hand it to your potential customer. I guarantee he'll be happy to keep it and may even give you a call.

The Head Boxer

M y good friend Ron Frame recommended that I include this very amusing stage or platform effect. It can actually be performed in any fairly large room. The only prop is a medium-sized cardboard box. Any flaps on the open side should be cut away. On one side, a square should be cut away so that when the box is placed on your assistant's shoulders, his head can be easily seen. And now you know the exact size of the box. It must be of a size so that its open side will rest easily on your partner's shoulders (Illus. 159).

Have your assistant sit in a chair, facing the group. "Ladies and gentlemen, may I introduce the fabulous Contorto the Twister. He can maneuver every portion of his body in ways that seem absolutely impossible. Tonight, Contorto will give us one small sample of his art. It is far too exhausting for him to do more."

Turn to your assistant. "Are you ready, Contorto?"

Yes, he is.

Pick up the box and place it on Contorto's shoulders, saying, "We're going to use this box, ladies and gentlemen, both to help *twist his head* and to conceal the ugly sight of his horribly painful expression as he performs his magnificent feat. Watch!"

Stand behind Contorto and a bit to one side so that all can see the front of the box. Begin to turn the box clockwise. As you do, Contorto turns his head to the right as far as he can. Apparently, the box is actually turning his head. As you continue turning the box, the audience sees the left side of the box and then the back of the box.

Meanwhile, as soon as his head was out of sight, your assistant turned his head as far as he could to the left and assumed a very painful expression. When your assistant looks directly at the hole on the left side, he starts moving his head to the right. Naturally, he matches the movement of the box. When the hole and his head reach the front, Contorto stops moving his head and lets out a groan of relief.

You pause a moment and then whip the box off his head. Immediately, Contorto shakes his head and rubs his neck. Oh! the agony.

214

Gesture toward your assistant, saying, "The great Contorto the Twister, ladies and gentlemen!"

You're very likely to get lively applause. It's very unlikely, however, that you will have actually fooled anyone. But the trick is clever and amusing, and, after all, the point is to entertain.

I'm sure I don't have to tell you that you and Contorto had better practice as long as it takes to get the timing down perfectly.

Illus. 159

Mental Magic

Mental magic primarily deals with precognition and telepathy. Making predictions can be considered precognition, and mind reading can be considered a form of telepathy. Every good magician when performing these tricks pretends to have these mental powers. Some pretend with great seriousness, and others are not nearly as serious. My preference is to present each trick with a feigned solemnity, but with a bit of a twinkle in the eye. And at the denouement, I am every bit as surprised as the spectators. How in the world did this mental miracle occur?

You, of course, will perform mental tricks according to your personality. It's best, however, to keep a middle ground. It's probably advisable not to make a complete mockery of a mental trick; on the other hand, nothing is worse than a pompous pretense to a real psychic ability.

Whichever tricks you choose, and however you wish to perform them, there is a wondrous collection here.

Something to Sniff At

Many excellent mind-reading tricks depend on the assistance of a confederate. It goes without saying that this person should not be suspected.

Howard P. Albright developed an extremely clever use of an "unknown assistant."

Let's assume that a fair-sized group is gathered in a living room or perhaps a recreation room. You announce, "I'd like to try an experiment in mind reading. In this instance, I'll depend on the mental vibrations from this entire group to lead me to a freely chosen object."

If you're good at it, you may wish to continue speaking in this vein for a bit. Eventually, add, "But first of all, I must be blindfolded." Remove a handkerchief from your pocket and fold it so that it looks as shown in Illus. 160. Ask someone to cover your eyes with it and tie it at the back of your head.

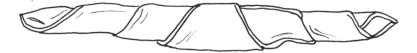

Illus. 160

Regardless of who ties it, you'll be able to look down and see the floor and quite a bit more. Make sure you don't reveal this to the audience. Your best bet is to keep your eyes closed until you need to do some surreptitious peeking.

"In a moment, someone will lead me out of the room. While I'm gone, I'd like you all to decide on a particular object in the room. When I come back, I'll try to find that object. Send someone to let us know when you're ready."

Have someone lead you from the room. Remember to keep your eyes shut!

When the group is ready, you're led back into the room. Ask your leader to take you to the middle of the room.

Tell the group, "Please concentrate on the object as I move about the room. And keep very quiet; I don't want you to give me any hints as to how I'm doing."

Oh, you rascal! Of course, you want to be given hints. And your confederate will oblige you.

You're standing in the middle of the room. Very slowly turn in a circle. Your accomplice, Thelma, gives a sniff when you face the proper direction. Slowly, tentatively, you move in the indicated direction. You can keep from hurting yourself by looking down your cheeks to see where you're going.

Now as you move, turn slowly from side to side. When you hear another sniff, you know that you're heading in the right direction. If you hear *no* sniff, you must turn in another direction. Let's say that the sniffs direct you to a table. As you slowly pass your hand over the objects on the table, another sniff will tell you that you are *hot.*

Many times, you'll find the exact object. But it doesn't really matter. Let's suppose that you've been guided to an area, but have no idea what the actual object could possibly be. You say, "I feel drawn to this area, just as though I've been pulled by a magnet. But I can't figure out exactly what it is."

You might ask what the selected object is. "Exactly! I should have known. Let's try again."

The whole experiment can be repeated. You may very well get the exact object. But it's still pretty amazing if you only get close.

Note: If possible, practice with your accomplice. You'll be pleased with the degree of accuracy attained after an hour's rehearsal. Surprisingly enough, however, quite often you'll hit the mark on a first try.

To Aid and Abet

The group is seated in your living room, eagerly awaiting your next demonstration of extrasensory perception. You place a key or another small object on an end table, saying, "While I'm out of the room, I'd like one of you to pick up this object and put it in your pocket, or sit on it, or conceal it on or near your person in some other way. Don't call me back. I'll return in approximately one minute." (If you prefer, you may ask that someone come up and hold the object briefly so that "it will be imprinted with that individual's personality.")

You leave the room. When you return, look carefully at each person, obviously concentrating, perhaps looking for certain signs from the person who has the key.

Soon you identify that person, much to the amazement of all. The stunt may be repeated a few times if you desire, and if *they* desire.

Once more you've used a confederate, you sneaky rascal. Let's say that Thelma is your confederate again. As you look the group over, you note how Thelma is seated. The person holding the key is seated in exactly the same way. If Thelma has her legs crossed, so has the person with the key. If Thelma has her arms folded, so has the key-holder.

Be sure to try this; it's a real fooler and absurdly easy to do.

Note: It has been suggested that you may wish to use an object like a spoon. Place it on the table and ask that, while you're out of the room, someone simply hold the object for a moment and then replace it on the table. When you return to the room, you examine the object minutely—turn it every which way, rub it, hold it up to the light. Finally, you figure out who must have held it.

I Have a Title

British magician Stephen Tucker invented this wonderful book test. The trick is clever, deceptive, and has a bit of humor that creates a strong climax.

By way of preparation, you'll need only a few file cards, a pen, and assorted books. If you are at someone else's house and the books are at hand, all the better. On one side of one of the file cards, print this: THE TITLE OF THE (Illus. 161).

To start, casually show the two file cards, making sure no one can see that something is written on one. Dixie is bright and cooperative, so she's the perfect subject for this test. Say to her, "Dixie, I'm going to make a prediction." Hold up the two file cards so that the part you have written on previously is facing you. "I'm going to put down the word which you'll think of. I hope." Again, make sure no one else can see the words as you print this below the previous printing: CHOSEN BOOK (Illus. 162).

Place this card print side down on the table. Place a small object such as a glass or vase on top of it.

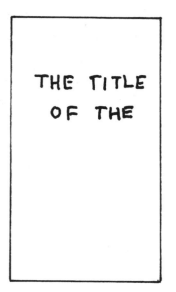

Illus. 161

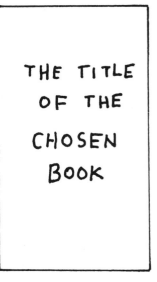

Illus. 162

222

"Dixie, in a moment I'll turn my back. When I do, I'd like you to select any of these books. Open that book to any page. Look over the page until some word seems to leap out at you. That will be your chosen word. So please remember it. Then close the book and set it with the others so that I won't know which one you chose. Clear?" If not, explain further.

You turn away. After Dixie has finished, turn back and say, "I believe that my prediction has been successful. Dixie, would you please announce the word that seemed to get your attention."

She does so. Nod. "Well, I was close." Immediately add, "Now, let's see if I can write down the title of the chosen book." Pick up the pen and the blank filing card. Pretend to print extensively, pausing and thinking. Actually, you write down a variation of the chosen word. For instance, if the chosen word were *soup*, you might write down *soap*. If the chosen word were *intimate*, you might write down *imitate*. The idea is to write down a word that can be immediately identified as *almost* correct. Stephen Tucker indicates that this is much more effective than putting down the exact correct word, and I've found this to be true.

Slip this card under the glass with the other card. Now you chat with the group, creating a bit of "time misdirection," giving them a chance to forget the exact situation with the cards. You might say, "Once in a while, I actually come close to getting the right words. But it's extremely difficult trying to get the title of the chosen book." As you're talking, you take the cards from beneath the glass. Casually toss aside for the moment the card with the selected word on it. "Let's see how I did. What book did you use, Dixie?" She tells you. "And I said that I'd print the title of the chosen book."

Show the card on which you printed the words: THE TITLE OF THE CHOSEN BOOK. You will get some appreciative chuckles, if not actual laughter.

The above segment of the trick is completely disarming and sets up the group for the climax.

Toss the card aside and pick up the other card, keeping the printing concealed. "Remember, Dixie, I said that I'd put down *the word which you'll think of*." You emphasize the phrase to make sure everyone expects you to repeat the joke with the book title.

"What word did you think of, Dixie?" Let's suppose her word was *amble*. "As I say, I came pretty close." Turn the card around, showing that you printed out *amiable* (or something similar).

Note: As you probably know, you pre-print THE TITLE OF THE so that you won't have to print too much when you are presumably putting down the prediction word.

Play the Odds

Playing cards are perfect for mental magic, so the remaining tricks in this section are all done with cards.

I believe that this is a more convincing version of a trick I previously published. The other involved slips of paper and provided the spectator few options; this one involves playing cards and gives the spectator many choices.

"I'll need a card for every digit," you comment as you fan through the cards and toss onto the table the ace through ten of any suit (A 2 3 4 5 6 7 8 9 10).

Set the rest of the deck aside. Gather up the cards you tossed out. Give them a little shuffle. Hold the cards up in a fan with the faces toward you. Say to Jerry, "Please take out one card, Jerry, and put it face down on the table." It doesn't matter whether he looks at the card or not. You, however, make it a point to see what the card is.

Here are the various card combinations that belong together:

A-2 3-4 5-6 7-8 9-10

So you pick out the card that goes with the one that Jerry placed face down on the table. Place this card face up on top of Jerry's selection. Let's suppose that Jerry placed the 8 face down on the table. You pick out the 7 and put it face up on top of the 8.

Jerry picks out another card and puts it face down onto the table. Again, you put the appropriate card face up on top of it.

Continue this until five back-to-back sets are on the table.

You will always pick out the correct card because you'll remember that *the odd card is always lower than the even card.* Thus, if Jerry selects an even card, like the 6, you know that the matching card is one card lower—the 5. Let's say that Jerry picks the 7, an odd card. You know that the paired card must be higher; therefore, place the 8 face down on top of it.

After matching the cards, turn away and give Jerry these instructions: "Pick up those pairs in any order you want, Jerry. The idea is to turn them into one pile. If you want, you can turn over some pairs as you gather them up."

When he's ready, continue, with appropriate pauses: "You can turn the pile over or not, as you wish. Give the pile a complete cut. And give it another complete cut. Keep doing that until you see a face-up card on top. Now fan out the top two cards and turn them over on top.

"You can turn the packet over if you wish. And you can cut the packet and keep cutting until you see another face-up card on top. Now fan out the top two cards and turn them over on top.

"Turn the packet over. Now, deal out an even number of cards into a pile—wait a second!—but turn each card over as you deal it. Now, either put those cards back on top or drop the rest of the cards in your hand on top of them."

After the cards have been sufficiently "mixed," continue: "Jerry, cut the cards until a face-up card is on top. Next, fan out the top two cards and put them onto the table. Do the same with the next two cards, putting them somewhere else on the table. Continue putting the pairs on the table in different spots. As you place a pair down, turn it over if you wish."

When he's done, say, "I'll try to figure out what the total is that's showing." You concentrate fiercely, but to no avail. "Maybe this will help. So far, everything we've done has been with even numbers. Let's see how odd we can get. Tell me, Jerry, how many of the cards that are showing are odd— you know, ace, three, five, seven, nine?"

He tells you, but you still have trouble guessing the correct number. At last you remember to subtract the number of odd cards from 30. This gives you the total of the face-up cards.

For instance, Jerry tells you that three odd cards are showing. You subtract 3 from 30, and know that the face-up cards total 27.

To repeat, face the group and have Jerry gather up the pairs one on top of the other. You face the group because you want to make sure he doesn't mix the cards. Then have Jerry, or some other spectator, go through the same procedure as before.

After the cards are placed down in pairs on different parts of the table, you again can't seem to get the total of the face-up cards. "We tried to be odd last time. This time, let's even things up. How many of the face-up cards are even?"

When told this number, subtract it from 5, giving you the number of odd cards that are face up. As before, you subtract the odd number of cards from 30.

Suppose that only one even card is turned face up. You subtract 1 from 5, giving you 4 odd cards. Then subtract 4 from 30, getting the total of the face-up cards, which is 26.

Note: Here are the options you provide Jerry. You can have him perform any or all of them as often as you wish:

(1) Give the packet a complete cut.

(2) With a face-up card on top, fan out the top two cards and turn them over.

(3) With a face-up card on top, deal out an even number of cards into a pile, turning each card over as it is dealt. This pile may be placed on top of the remainder in your hand, or you may place the cards in your hand on top of the other.

Remember: After Jerry turns over two cards, there's still

a face-up card on top. If you direct Jerry to turn the pile over, there will still be a face-up card on top. So at this point you can direct Jerry to perform either (2) or (3). Clearly, no trick is more readily available than one using only the hands. The first four tricks here can be combined, forming a miniroutine. The fifth can be used as a humorous introduction to the routine, or for that matter, as an introduction to tricks with handkerchiefs.

With the first four tricks, it's wise to check the various moves in the mirror to make sure that you have everything just right.

The remaining tricks and stunts require little or no practice, as you'll see.

Hands

Clearly, no trick is more readily available than one using only the hands. The first four tricks here can be combined, forming a miniroutine. The fifth can be used as a humorous introduction to the routine, or for that matter, as an introduction to tricks with handkerchiefs.

With the first four tricks, it's wise to check the various moves in the mirror to make sure that you have everything just right.

The remaining tricks and stunts require little or no practice, as you'll see.

A Longer Finger

Here we have a combination of optical illusion and subtle trickery. In many respects, this is the best trick in the section.

Hold up the first finger of your left hand, declaring, "I'm going to make every effort to stretch this finger. But don't expect miracles; it may stretch out only an inch or two."

Place the finger on your right leg, bending it up somewhat (Illus. 163). Place your right first finger on top, a bit

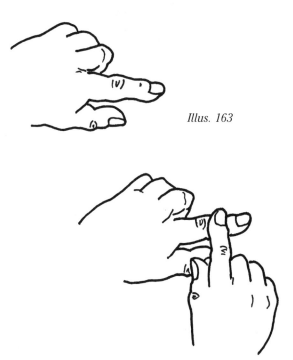

Illus. 163

Illus. 164

below the fingernail (Illus. 164).

Move your right first finger rapidly back and forth along the left first finger, from the bottom portion of the fingernail to the second joint (Illus. 165). As you do so, gradually push down on the left first finger so that it extends to its maximum length. This must be done over a period of at least ten seconds. Also, and this is of great importance, as you push the first finger out, bring the visible portion of the other three fingers back and under. Compare Illus. 164 and 165 to see what I mean.

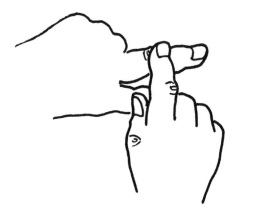

Illus. 165

Two things happen: (1) The back-and-forth motion creates an illusion of the finger lengthening. (2) The extension of the finger to its maximum length actually makes it longer.

As you smoothly combine the elements, it may even seem to you that the finger is growing longer.

Finger Stretch

In the description of this trick, it may seem to you that the fingers must be contorted. Not so! I couldn't possibly perform a trick that would call for unusual stretches of the fingers. But I can do this trick perfectly. And so can you. Give it a try.

Implied in all descriptions of this trick is that the positioning of the fingers must be done in advance, with no witnesses. I've devised a wrinkle that enables you to proceed with everyone watching.

If you're doing a routine, you might begin like this: "You've just seen me stretch out the first finger on my *left* hand. Let's see if I can do an even better job with the first finger on my *right* hand."

Otherwise, you can begin with a comment like this: "When the weather is just right, I can actually stretch my first finger. Watch!"

While speaking, display the first finger of your right hand and waggle it (Illus. 166). Bend over and bring both hands down to hip level. If you bend your hands back toward your body, no one can see what you're up to.

And here's what you *are* up to: Put your right first finger on top of your left first finger so that it covers the second

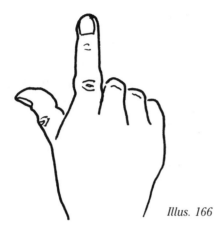

Illus. 166

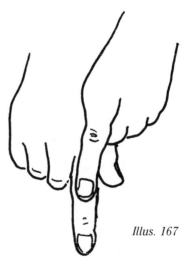

Illus. 167

234

joint (Illus. 167). Now put your left second finger over the right first finger so that the first finger's nail is covered (Illus. 168). (Try this out. Now go to a mirror and take a look while doing this. Pretty good, eh?)

As you do the preceding move, grunt as though in pain. "That *hurts* when you stretch it. Maybe I stretched it too far. What do you think?"

Bring your hands up to waist level, displaying your stretched finger. Let everyone get a good look.

To finish, just "ram" your right first finger between the first and second fingers of your left hand (Illus. 169). Twist it around for a bit. Then pull it out and hold it up. Exhale in relief.

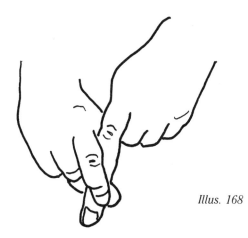

Illus. 168

"Ah, that's better."

Rubber Fingers

"**P**erhaps you've noticed how good I am at stretching things—fingers, thumbs... the truth. You name it, I'll stretch it. If you've wondered how I'm able to do so many fabulous tricks with my digits, I'll be happy to explain."

As you make this last statement, hold up your hands and wiggle your fingers.

"The fact is, I happen to be extremely lucky. You see, I have rubber fingers. Watch!"

Hold your hands together in a praying position. The following actions are performed very rapidly. Leaning the hands slightly to your left, move the right hand up over the left, wrapping the right fingers over the left fingers.

Then, leaning the hands slightly to the right, move the left hand up over the right, wrapping the left fingers over the right fingers. Continue alternating this move rapidly and without stopping. Perform it at least six times on each side. (I mentally count to 12, adding one for each time I make the basic move.)

Check it out in a mirror. The illusion is that your fingers are indeed extraordinarily rubbery.

Snap Your Finger

Y ou "break off" a finger and then restore it. Ken de Courcy invented this very clever method.

The digit you're going to break off is your left middle finger. Start with your left hand held up palm inward, with the fingers spread wide apart and pointing upward.

With the right hand, approach the left from above, fingers pointing down. Also, the right fingers are cupped, almost clawlike.When the right hand obscures the view of the audience, bend back the left middle finger so that the tip almost rests in the left palm. (Make sure that the right thumb is held back to clear the way for the left middle finger.)

Apparently grip the top portion of the left middle finger with the clawlike right fingers in front and the thumb in back. The left fingers on either side are spread out so that the audience has a good view of the grip.

With a sudden sharp movement, bend the right hand forward, as though breaking off the middle finger. At the same time, make a loud crackling noise with your mouth.

Hold your right hand up, back to the audience, apparently holding the detached digit. Hold the left hand fairly close to the body so that no one can get a side view.

"It's easy enough for a lunatic to break off one of his

fingers," you explain, "but it takes a crazy magician to restore it."

Bring the right hand over the left as before and apparently put the finger back on the left hand. Naturally, when the left hand covers the opening left by the missing finger, you straighten out that finger. (Again, make sure the thumb is held back and out of the way to allow clearance for the left middle finger.) The concluding move is to slide your right hand upward and off the restored finger.

Magic Finger

Tricks don't get much dumber than this one. Just whip out your handkerchief and begin.

Hold the handkerchief by two adjacent corners, letting it hang down. With grand flourishes, show both sides of the handkerchief.

"And now, ladies and gentlemen, a magical appearance. I present for your viewing enjoyment a magical illusion which has defied the understanding of some of the greatest magicians in the world. Mainly, they can't understand why I keep doing it."

Hold up the right fist with its back to the audience. Cover the fist with the handkerchief. Make several magical gestures over the handkerchief with your left hand. Pop up the first finger of the right hand so that it suddenly pushes up the handkerchief. Pause for a moment. Then with the left hand grab a corner of the handkerchief and pull it off. Proudly display the extended right first finger. Once more, show both sides of the handkerchief.

Bang!

You must be able to snap your fingers to perform this stunt.

Using your best gangster dialect, address Martin, a mighty good sport: "All right, you dirty rat, you've gone too far this time. You asked for it, and now you're gonna get it."

Point your left first finger at Martin, pretending that it's the barrel of a gun. The other fingers are folded in, and the thumb is parallel to the first finger. With your right first finger, lift the left thumb back, as though cocking a gun.

Move the "gun" abruptly forward, as though firing a shot. At the same time, snap your right thumb against your middle finger, making a sharp noise.

Most will wonder where the noise is coming from. Do a quick repeat.

Up the Ladder

"I have been studying the techniques of firemen and of great mountain climbers, and now I can climb anything with extraordinary speed. I'll demonstrate how fast I can go."

Your hands are together at about stomach level. With the right first finger touch the pad of the left thumb. Retaining contact, turn the right hand clockwise, and the left counterclockwise, revolving the finger on the left thumb and bringing the right thumb up to the left first finger.

Next, revolve the right hand counterclockwise and the left clockwise, as you bring the right first finger up to the left thumb—the starting position. Repeat these movements extremely rapidly. As you do, raise the hands bit by bit until your arms are extended to full length over your head.

Drop your hands, exhaling sharply. "I'm exhausted."

Spectators usually find the climbing action quite intriguing.

The Swinging Arm

This maneuver was a favorite of that hilarious silent Marx brother, Harpo. He would swing his arm around as though his elbow were a rubber band. You, too, can perform this feat, but it will require a bit of practice in front of a mirror.

To get the correct starting position, you should hold your left arm out to your left, so that it is shoulder high. Now bend it at the elbow, forming a right angle, the fingers pointing at the floor. The back of the hand is toward the audience.

Ready? With the right hand, grasp the left fingers and pull them to the right several inches. Release the left fingers. Make the lower left arm go back and forth like a pendulum. Do this a few times.

The next portion, practiced and done properly, creates the illusion that the left arm bends in an absolutely impossible way. As described above, your upper left arm is extended from the shoulder and the lower left arm is at right angles to it, with fingers pointing down. With your right hand, grasp the left hand, as before. Pull it to the right a bit and then give it a little push to the left.

The lower arm pivots in a complete clockwise circle, returns to its original position, and then swings back and forth in gradually smaller arcs.

How do you do it? At one point in the circle, the left arm is extended straight out. At this point, turn your left hand palm outward. The hand continues around 180 degrees and is somewhere near your chin. At this point, turn your left hand palm inward again. The whole circular movement must be quite rapid, and the revolving arm must be kept on a *flat plane*.

The illusion is quite startling. It's probably best not to do a repeat until another occasion.

As the Spirit Moves

At a party, you might declare, "I feel the presence of a ghost in this house. Anyone else have that feeling?"

Millie probably has the same feeling, so say to her, "Good. Then maybe we can demonstrate that the ghost is actually here."

You face each other, sides to the group, and as far away from the group as possible. "I'd like to try a test to see if you *really* feel the presence of the ghost. Now everyone else has to promise not to try any funny business, okay?"

The group agrees.

Say to Millie, "As you know, ghosts don't particularly like to be seen, so I will need you to close your eyes. Not yet! You'll want to know where my hands are at all times, so I'll use them to help you keep your eyes closed. Stand very still, please."

Bring your two hands up, first fingers extended toward Millie. Slowly move your hands toward her eyes. When you're an inch or two away, she will close her eyes. When she does, place the first finger and second finger of one hand on her eyelids, pressing *very, very gently*.

"Good heavens!" you declare. "I see a vague figure floating above us."

Flick her hair with the fingers of your free hand. Ask her, "Did you feel it?"

You can quickly perform other ghostly deeds, like tapping her wrist, snapping your fingers near her ear, placing something on her head. You might take out your keys, for instance, saying, "Hey, put that back! It's got my keys." Then place the keys onto her head.

After several quick stunts, extend the first finger of your free hand and move the hand just in front of her eye. Withdraw the two fingers from her eyes, instantly folding in your second finger, so that you're back into the original position. As you remove your fingers from her eyes, say, "You can open your eyes now."

After making sure Millie has a good look at your hands, drop them to your sides.

"Whoops! the ghost is gone."

Usually, while the ghost is manifesting itself, the group will join in, indicating they can see the ghost.

In all likelihood, the only problem you'll have is convincing your subject that no one else in the group participated.

Occasionally, your subject will pull away, opening her eyes. Quickly drop both hands to your sides and look as innocent as you possibly can.

Numbers

One key to effective number magic is to minimize the fact that you're using numbers; for example, say to the audience, "To make sure that we choose a number completely at random, we'll just… "

In a book test, you might say, "We'll need to choose a page and a word on that page. So that you won't think that in some way psychology is used to force a selection, we'll have you choose a page by… "

Another key is to make the trick so entertaining that the use of numbers becomes something of a minor circumstance.

The first four tricks below provide quite a variety of approaches. The remaining five enable you to perform astonishing number tricks with a calendar.

Mathematical Book Test

Pierre Fontaine, I believe, developed this trick based on a principle developed by Ron Frost. The principle is quite simple, but the handling can turn the trick into a miracle.

By way of preparation, you should have at least 12 slips of paper. Every slip will have a different number on each side. For instance, one slip might have 97 on one side and 48 on the other. Another might have 64 on one side and 81 on the other. The slips will have only one thing in common: The two sides add up to 145. Make sure that you don't use any number more than once.

You'll also need some paper, a pencil, and a book.

Ready? Announce to the group, "I'd like to perform a book test." Hold up the book. "You'll choose a page and a word on that page. Someone here will concentrate on that word. In the past I've had some luck at actually figuring out what that word might be. Let's see if I'm as lucky this time."

Toss the slips of paper onto the table. "Here we have 12 slips of paper. Each one has numbers on both sides. I'd like you to examine them. You'll notice that no two slips are alike."

Get three different spectators to choose a slip. Pick up the rest and put them into your pocket.

Since Jane is superb at addition, she would make a perfect additional volunteer. Hand her the paper and pencil.

Turn away and address Jane: "Collect the three slips, please, Jane, and put them into a pile. Put down the numbers that are on one side of the slips, please, and add them up."

When she's done, continue: "Now, turn the slips over

and, in a separate spot, put down the numbers on the other side of the slips and add them up." Pause. "You now have two different totals. Please add these totals together."

The result will always be 435 (3 times 145).

It's time for a psychological ploy. "How many digits are there, Jane?"

Three.

"Good. Pick up the book, please. Now, use the first digit or, if you prefer, the first two digits to find a page. Turn to that page." She does. "Now, use the remaining digit, or the remaining two digits, to count to a word on that page. Just start with the first word and move from left to right. If need be, go to the next line and keep on going—line after line. Tell me when you're ready."

When she's ready, you know absolutely whether she chose page 4 and word 35, or page 43 and word 5. First, it would take her quite a bit longer to find page 43. Second, it would take her *much* longer to count to word 35.

And because you're well prepared, you know the 5th word on page 43 and the 35th word on page 4.

Your back is still turned to the group. "Please put the slips into my hand." She does. Crumple them in one hand and then hold that hand at the side of your head. She concentrates, and you concentrate. Eventually, you name the word or, for verisimilitude, a word that closely resembles it.

Notes:

(1) I choose to have the spectator end with the number 435 because these particular digits make it easy to figure out what her page and word numbers are. But you may try out other numbers easily enough. If you want the spectator to choose a particular word, for instance, you could make the sides of each slip total 138. This would yield an eventual total of 414 (3 times 138). The first two digits could be the page and the last digit the word number on the first line of that page.

(2) Here's another possibility: Using the selected number (in our example 435), you could have the spectator use the first digit for the page number, the second for the line, and the third for a word in that line. You could have your slips total 183, yielding 549. This would give you page 5, line 4, and word number 9 on that line.

Multiple Choice

"**I** used to be really good at multiplication," you explain to Shirley. "I wonder if I still am. Between us, let's make up an easy multiplication problem. First, you put down any two-digit number."

Let's say that Shirley jots down 47.

"Now, I'll put down a two-digit number."

You construct your number like this: Your first digit is the same as Shirley's first digit. Your second digit adds up to 10 with Shirley's second digit. In other words, you subtract Shirley's second digit from 10 to get your second digit. Her second digit is 7. 10 - 7 = 3. So your second digit is 3. Your two-digit number is 43.

"Let's see how fast I can multiply it."

$$47$$
$$\text{x } 43$$

You draw a line beneath the two numbers and *immediately* jot down your answer. When Shirley does her multiplication, it turns out that you're absolutely correct.

Here's what you do: You mentally add 1 to Shirley's first digit and then multiply it by *your* first digit. Shirley's first digit is 4; add 1 to it and you get 5. Your first digit is also 4. Multiply 5 by 4 and you get 20. So jot down 20 to the left:

$$47$$
$$\text{x } 43$$
$$20$$

Now, multiply Shirley's second digit by your second digit. 7 x 3 = 21. Enter this to the right of the previous entry:

$$47$$
$$\text{x } 43$$
$$2021$$

Let's try another example. Suppose Shirley puts down this two-digit number: 83. Your two-digit number will begin with an 8, the same as Shirley's first digit. You subtract Shirley's second digit (3) from 10 to get your second digit. 10 - 3 = 7. So your second digit is 7. Your two-digit number is 87.

$$83$$
$$\text{x } 87$$

You draw a line beneath the two numbers and go to work. Add 1 to Shirley's first digit, making it 9. Multiply this by your first digit. 9 x 8 = 72. So put 72 down on the left:

$$83$$
$$\text{x } 87$$
$$72$$

Next, multiply Shirley's second digit by your second digit. 3 x 7 = 21. Put this to the right of the previous entry:

$$83$$
$$\text{x } 87$$
$$7221$$

And, quick as a wink, you have your answer.

All the Same

T his magic square uses a principle that I've previously adapted to a card trick in my book Mystifying Card

Tricks. The basic idea is this: Multiply 142,857 by any number from 1 to 6 and you will end up with precisely the same digits as in the original number. Obviously, with each multiplier, you end up with the digits in a different order.

You'll have no trouble remembering these numbers if you'll remember "unfortunate 57," or "un - for - tune - ate 57 (varieties)."

1	4	2	8	5	7
un	for	tune	ate	fifty	seven

By way of preparation, you'll need six slips of paper and six pencils for spectators. And you'll need another pencil and a sheet of paper for yourself. On your sheet of paper, draw a blank six-by-six grid (Illus. 170). At the top of each slip of paper, you should write your six-digit number, 142,857, so that each slip looks like Illus. 171.

Elicit the aid of six persons. Hand each of them a pencil and a slip of paper with the number on top.

"Let's start by having a number chosen at random." Address Adelle, one of the volunteers: "How about choosing a fairly high number... say, something in the thirties."

She names a number, let's say 35. "Good. Now, add the digits in 35 and what do you get?" She gets 8. "Subtract that from your original number and what do you have?" She has

Illus. 170

142,857

Illus. 171

27. In fact, any number she names in the thirties will yield 27.

"Twenty-seven! We'll have to remember that. Now it's time for hard work. I will give each of you a different number from one to six."

Give out the numbers in order, starting at your left. "You'll notice that you have a number at the top of your paper. I'd like each of you to multiply that number by the digit that I gave you."

After the multiplication is done, invite all to watch as you enter the results in your magic square. "Who wants to give me the result first?"

Adelle volunteers—the little show-off. "All right. Your answer will be put down in one of these six columns. Which one do you choose?"

Let's assume that she chooses the second column from the left. Further, let's assume that the digit she multiplied by is 3. Have her read you her answer one digit at a time. Enter it in the appropriate column as she dictates (Illus. 172).

4					
2					
8					
5					
7					
1					

Illus. 172

The remaining spectators in turn choose a column and read their answer. You enter each answer in the selected column. One possible result is shown in Illus. 173.

1	4	2	8	5	7
4	2	8	5	7	1
2	8	5	7	1	4
8	5	7	1	4	2
5	7	1	4	2	8
7	1	4	2	8	5

Illus. 173

At the end, hand the sheet to Adelle. "Please add any column, Adelle, and tell us what you get."

She does. "Ah, 27—the number that you chose at the beginning. Add another column, Adelle."

Once more she gets 27. When you ask her to add any row, she also gets 27.

"In fact," you point out, "each and every column and row adds up to your selected number—27. How did you do that, Adelle?"

Triple Dates

This trick is quite simple, and spectators may even have an inkling of how you do it. But the one that follows, *Quadruple Dates,* is a dazzling display of your calculating ability. In both tricks, you use a calendar and pen.

Hand the calendar and pen to Denise and turn your back. "Denise, I'd like you to put a circle around three consecutive numbers on a line. Then add these numbers together."

When she's done, you ask, "What's the total?"

She tells you, and you immediately name the three numbers.

The method is absurdly simple. You divide by 3 to get the middle number, and then give the number immediately preceding it, the middle number itself, and the number after it.

Denise has circled, let's say, numbers 13, 14, 15. She adds them together and tells you the result: 42. You divide by 3, giving you 14. So you proudly announce, "The numbers you circled were 13, 14, and 15."

While the method seems very obvious to us, onlookers are usually fooled. Nevertheless, proceed immediately to the next feat.

Quadruple Dates

We are not exactly getting into higher math with this stunt, but it's a real fooler all the same. You could perform this as straight mind reading, but I think it works better as an example of how rapidly your mind works.

Hand John a calendar and a pen. "John, let's try a test of how quickly I can make certain computations." Turn your back and say, "I'd like you to pick out any calendar page. Don't tell me which month you pick. Please use your pen and surround four dates with a square. That is, enclose two dates on one line and the two dates just below them. Then add up the four dates and tell me the total."

Let's assume that John tells you the total is 64. You quickly name the four dates he has circled. How? A glance at a calendar will reveal that all that has to be done is to find the *first date* of the four, and you can derive the others. You get the first date by dividing by 4, and then subtracting 4. In our example, you divide 64 by 4, giving you 16. Subtract 4 from 16, and you get 12. So 12 is the first date.

If you look at Illus. 174, the rest is obvious. You announce 12 and the next higher number, 13. You mentally add 7 to the first date, 12, giving you 19, which you announce. And then you announce the next-higher number after 19, which is 20.

Actually, once you have divided by 4 and subtracted 4, the rest goes very rapidly. Almost immediately, you announce, "12, 13, 19, 20."

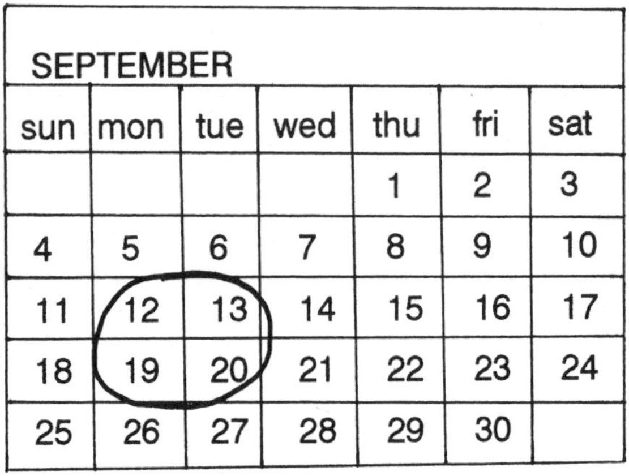

SEPTEMBER						
sun	mon	tue	wed	thu	fri	sat
				1	2	3
4	5	6	7	8	9	10
11	12	13	14	15	16	17
18	19	20	21	22	23	24
25	26	27	28	29	30	

Illus. 174

Review: The spectator forms a square around four numbers on a calendar. He adds the numbers within the square and tells you the total. You divide by 4 and subtract 4. This reveals the first number. Add 1 to it for the second number. Add 7 to the first number for your third number. Now add 1 to the third number for your last number.

You can repeat this one several times.

One of Our Dates Is Missing 1

Evelyn received an A in high school algebra, so she should be perfect for this trick.

As usual, you present her with a calendar. She will also need a pen or pencil and perhaps a sheet of paper.

Turn your back and tell her, "Please pick out a month in which a particular day appears five times."

When she has one, continue: "You have found a day which appears five times, right?" Right. "So please circle the first two dates under that day. And then circle the last two dates under that day."

Makes sure Evelyn understands exactly what she is to do.

In Illus. 175, you'll find a typical choice.

JULY						
sun	mon	tue	wed	thu	fri	sat
			1	②	3	4
5	6	7	8	⑨	10	11
12	13	14	15	16	17	18
19	20	21	22	㉓	24	25
26	27	28	29	㉚	31	

Illus. 175

"Now add up all the circled days."

She does.

"What's your total?"

Evelyn tells you. She might, for instance, say, "Sixty-four."

Furrow your brow and announce, "The number you did *not* circle in that column is sixteen."

All are aghast, not realizing how quickly you can divide big numbers by 4. That's right. Evelyn gives you a number, and you divide it by 4.

Possibly you'll be cheered to know that there are only three possible totals: 68, 64, and 60. And the correct answers are 17, 16, and 15, respectively.

Nothing to it.

One of Our Dates Is Missing 2

E velyn seems to have the hang of it, so let's try her on a similar trick. "Evelyn, please find another calendar page in which there's at least one day with five dates below it. Find one? Good. Now, look down that column of five numbers and circle the lowest number."

Pause.

"All you have to do now, Evelyn, is add up the other four numbers in that column."

She does it.

"And what total did you get?"

She tells you. And you immediately tell her the value of the date she circled. You know something? You're really getting good.

But let's admit this: It wasn't really all that tough. Evelyn could give you only three possible totals: 46, 50, 54. And there are only three possible answers: 29, 30, or 31.

A total of 46 gives you 29.

A total of 50 gives you 30.

A total of 54 gives you 31.

Just remember that 50 gives you 30. Since they both end in zero, this should not be a problem.

If you're given a total *below* 50 (46, that is), the answer must be the lower possibility, 29.

If you're given a total *above* 50 (54, that is), the answer must be the higher possibility, 31.

Nearly Hypnotic Tricks

Clearly, tricks purporting to be examples of hypnotism can be performed seriously or with tongue in cheek. In either instance, the "experiments" are presented in straightforward fashion. In the latter case, you perform them with a twinkle in the eye.

Should you pretend to put your volunteer into a trance? I think not. Instead, you might try this: "My experience is that very often certain persons can be influenced to behave in certain unusual ways. Sometimes this can be the result of a muscular reaction; sometimes it can be psychological. Many believe that such unusual behavior is brought about through hypnotism. As we try these experiments, I'd like you to judge for yourself."

You can expand on this while performing the various tricks. If so inclined, you can accompany the trick with an occasional hypnotic gesture.

Some of these "surefire" stunts will sometimes fail. When this happens, explain that you're only experimenting, and that there's never a guarantee that any experiment will work.

The Mighty Thread

Wally will go along with almost anything, so ask him to lie on his back on the floor.

"Wally, I'm going to try to keep you on the floor, using nothing more than a piece of thread."

Display a piece of thread about 10 inches long.

"Don't get nervous, Wally, but I'm going to place a handkerchief over your face. Now, just lie there with your arms at your side with the palms up."

Hold the thread between your hands and press it against the bridge of his nose.

"Don't push with your arms or hands, Wally, but see if you can sit up."

Even though you're using very little pressure, Wally will be unable to sit up. Let him try for several seconds and then take the thread away. He should be able to sit up easily.

The Power of Negative Thinking

Announce in a grandiose manner that you are psychic. "Not only that," you continue, "but I can hypnotize anyone else and make that person psychic."

Certainly there will be skeptics, but you should be able to get a volunteer. Assume Agnes is foolish enough to step forward. Wave your hands hypnotically in front of her eyes. "Soon you will be under my spell," you say, "and then you will be every bit as psychic as I am. Do you feel the power?"

Whatever she responds, say, "I know that you now have the power." Hold up a folded piece of paper. "Do you know what I have written on this paper?"

"No."

Open the paper and show that indeed Agnes is psychic, for you have printed NO on the paper in bold letters.

"See? You knew, you knew!"

Suppose your psychic friend does not answer no; suppose she says, "Uh-uh," or shakes her head. Say, "What?" Keep saying it until you get a correct response. Eventually you should. If you don't, ask someone else, "What is she trying to say?" You will probably get an emphatic "She's trying to say *no!*"

Open Your Eyes and Smell the Performer

S ince hypnosis has worked so well on Agnes, you might try this one.

"If you will allow me, I will hypnotize you once again."

Again, wave your hands hypnotically. "Now, you are under my spell. If you will be kind enough to close your eyes for me, I will *force* you to open them again."

As soon as she closes her eyes, say, "No, no, not that way."

Chances are overwhelming that Agnes will open her eyes immediately. "See? I told you I'd force you to open your eyes."

Straight from the Shoulder

L eon will probably be a good subject.

Explain to him, "Through some mysterious power, Leon, I'm going to force you to raise your arm, no matter how hard you try not to."

Have him extend his right arm straight out from the shoulder, palm up. "Now I'll work on raising your arm, perhaps just a little. Meanwhile, you try to hold your arm steady."

Make a hypnotic gesture or two if you wish. Then begin to stroke his extended hand very rapidly and gently. As you do so, press downward. Repeat the move at least ten times.

Perform the move a final time, except this time you don't

touch his hand. Instead, you pass your hand an inch or less above his palm and quickly withdraw.

If all goes well, in anticipation of your stroke, Leon will involuntarily push up.

Raise Your Hands

L ater, with Ted, you might try a stunt similar to Straight from the Shoulder.

Say, "Ted, please hold your hands out palms up." He does so. "Now I'm going to stroke your palms, and I'd like you to do what you can to keep your hands from being forced down. If I have the power, something very unusual may happen."

With the tips of your fingers, stroke his palms toward you several times. Take your hands away. Repeat the procedure, taking your hands away again. Place your hands over Ted's as though you're going to begin again, but don't touch his palms. Rather, continue the stroking motion as you slowly lift your hands.

As a rule, Ted's hands will rise, following your hands.

Nod. "I told you."

Please Stay Seated

L et's try something else with Ted.

"Ted, I'd like you to sit in this chair and lean your head back as far as you can." Gesture toward a straight-back chair.

Ted sits and leans his head back. At this time, you may posture hypnotically for a moment. "Whether you know it or not, Ted, you are now in my power. To you it will seem that my first finger has become enormously strong." Hold up your first finger for all to see and marvel at.

Place your finger on his forehead and press back. "Ted, I'd like you to try to stand up, but do not knock my finger away. I believe that you'll find it impossible."

It *is* impossible.

Remove your finger and gesture for him to rise. He does so with ease.

Mastery Levels Charts

Index